Leaving a Legacy

Jesus Christ and Others

Dr. David L. Clifton

WESTBOW
PRESS®
A DIVISION OF THOMAS NELSON
& ZONDERVAN

Cover image by Bobbyjo Birdsong Photography

WestBow Press books may be ordered through
booksellers or by contacting:

WestBow Press
A Division of Thomas Nelson & Zondervan
1663 Liberty Drive
Bloomington, IN 47403
www.westbowpress.com
1 (866) 928-1240

ISBN: 978-1-5127-2009-9 (sc)
ISBN: 978-1-5127-2010-5 (hc)
ISBN: 978-1-5127-2052-5 (e)

Library of Congress Control Number: 2015918906

Print information available on the last page.

WestBow Press rev. date: 11/17/2015

Contents

To Life Christian University

Submitted in partial fulfillment of the requirements for
the Doctor of Philosophy in Theology Degree Program
on December 01, 2004

Introduction

Throughout the course of history, humanity has left its imprint as an indelible mark upon the generations that followed. Some of humanity's most recognizable individuals have left their stamps by sheer force of their personalities, leaving a legacy of fame and power, recognition that has lasted throughout the ages. Others have engraved their names into the minds of generations simply by being at the right place at the right time.

One might call them sages, heroes, despots, tyrants, prophets, or great teachers, people whose illustrious lives in any period impacted the age in which they lived. Many exerted an irresistible pull on the minds and imaginations of thousands. Others, at the mere mention of their names, created fear and loathing among their critics and foes. Centuries have formed a composite of dictators, emperors, monarchs, schemers, warriors, philosophers, and disciples alike. All of these individuals meted out their influences in their turns, thereby determining what legacy they would leave.

History has proven that leaving a legacy is not easy. Many people lost their lives in trying to establish what they thought was best for those within their spheres of influence. Others' lives were taken as a result of the many conflicts they caused. All would have agreed that the venture demanded self-sacrifice, time, attention, and focus. Those whose lives were spared forged ahead. Whether they stood on the stage for only a brief moment or continued in successive acts, these participants were determined to leave an indication and remembrance of their own legacies. They all knew that an arduous task lay ahead. No matter how daunting it appeared at the time, those who bequeathed a legacy throughout history dispelled the challenges.

In the writings of the Greek biographer Plutarch, it is mentioned that Julius Caesar stood before the statue of Alexander the Great and wept. One can only speculate that he felt inadequate. Alexander, upon his death at the age of thirty-two, had conquered the known world. *Caesar* was the appellative taken by the many emperors of the Roman Empire, and the title remains recognizable throughout the world today.

In addition to individuals and leaders, empires, peoples, cultures, and various nationalities have extended their influences beyond the borders of their time to ensure that their legacies would last. From time immemorial to the present age, humans have toiled to secure a place in history so that they would not be forgotten. Conquering armies subjugated entire nations, guaranteeing that their own way of life dominated that of the vanquished foe. If the vanquisher proved to be especially hostile, the result would inevitably transform the hapless citizenry into compliant slaves. The governing power would eventually eradicate or forbid the overthrown inhabitants from flourishing further. Language, writing, and communication in general would no longer exist as it did prior to subjugation. Restrictions on movement were enforced, designed to control anyone deemed a traitor or insurgent. Whole villages, cities, and towns were leveled, with no trace left behind. Such was the inheritance of unfortunate protectorates. The leaders of aggressive powers set into motion the perpetuation of their own legacies of destruction.

A benevolent, autocratic government or hegemony, on the other hand, would enhance the structures of an acquired territory. If a mode of communication, for example, surpassed that which the conquering entity had, the conqueror would modify or adapt that system into its own working order. Both the Roman and British empires excelled at doing just that sort of thing. The legacies of both empires have stood the test of time. American structures set up by the Founding Fathers reflect the glory of Rome in governance while the British influence has been evident in numerous countries throughout the world. Aspects of both are entrenched into so many systems that it would leave an enormous void indeed if every governing element were to be removed. Both have proven to be beneficial in some areas.

Many cultures have left enduring legacies merely by following leaders who galvanized their every move. The Marquis de Lafayette had General George Washington as his mentor. Lafayette was such an ardent supporter of the general that he made a name for himself on the battlefields of the Revolutionary War. He has been memorialized in cities and villages throughout France and the United States.

Additionally, the name of Mahatma Gandhi has elicited fanatical support among his followers. Although Gandhi died decades ago, the family of Jawarharlal Nehru, the first prime minister of an independent India, managed to be elected simply by possessing the same last name as Gandhi. Nehru's daughter, Indira Gandhi, received her last name by marriage. It was often thought that she was related to the great Mahatma.

Having no connection to Mahatma Gandhi, she still served in office for many years before being assassinated. Likewise, her son, Rajiv Gandhi, was elected prime minister. He too was assassinated while running for reelection. His widow, Sonia Gandhi, has served as the leader of the Congress party since then. The name of Gandhi itself has proven to be a time-honored legacy. In India, all other names have paled in comparison.

Among all those who have traversed history, no legacy has proven as controversial yet enduring as that of Jesus Christ. During His short lifespan of thirty-three years on earth, He managed to appear before the authorities of that time, perform countless recorded miracles, and initiate followers who have since proliferated around the globe. It can be said that the legacy of Christ split the essence of time itself. By His mere existence, calendars around the world mark each passing year as AD, the acronym for the Latin *anno domini*. It is been commonly referred to as the time after the birth of Christ.

In the following chapters, we will see several examples of legacies left behind. We will show the impressions that remain of individuals, cultures, empires, disciples, and leaders of all kinds. We have included a comprehensive breadth of venues, seeking to be as inclusive as possible. We will attempt to assess what has been an advantage to humanity and what has proven detrimental. We will discuss what belief systems may have influenced people's actions and judgments, thereby determining their legacy. Finally, we will anchor all that is written and said with the life of Jesus Christ, proving that His is the greatest of all legacies.

1

The Legacy of Louis XIV

When one thinks of Louis XIV, the Palace of Versailles comes to mind immediately. We know that much more has been attributed to this great monarch of France than just a palace. But Versailles was no ordinary palace, and Louis XIV was no ordinary king. History testifies that France experienced its golden era during the reign of Louis XIV. Everything recorded about his reign described a monarchy more imposing than ever before in its history. Everything was done to exemplify and to magnify Louis. The magnification of such a personage served to glorify only one: the monarch of France.

Louis was aware of what he represented and did nothing to halt the accumulation of accolades during his reign. The glorification process so permeated French society and culture that anything less would have been seen as tantamount to treason. Some of this idolization may have been fueled by the introduction and vast development of arts, music, theater, and extravagant architectural structures. The crown paid those involved in the arts to assure that they "correctly" interpreted the legacy of Louis XIV. They produced an astounding array of paintings, buildings, and arts, all designed to lift ever higher the image of the great king of France. The eruption of activity astonished the world with the sheer number of projects undertaken. France became known as the artistic and cultural center of the world. Those employed by the court at Versailles also enjoyed obvious advantages.

In his book, *Louis XIV: A Royal Life*, Olivier Bernier makes the following observation: "The changes made by Louis XIV in the first year of his reign amounted to nothing less than a revolution" (p. 94). Indeed, Louis was not plagued by the same factors that the previous monarch had faced: a continuing war, grave financial obligations that drained the treasury, and the country's weakened political body, known as the Parliament. Louis was astute enough to seize the moment, consolidating his power and making a determined effort to establish his reign early on in 1661. Both Mazarin, Louis's manager of affairs, and his widowed mother, Anne of Austria, implanted in Louis a deep and penetrating awareness that he was ordained by God to serve. Louis fully believed that he represented God's will on earth.

Everything that Louis did revolved around this one core belief. His attitude became intransigent concerning the matters of state. It was even more pronounced where the church was involved. In Anthony Levi's book, *Louis XIV*, the author notes the following: "Louis felt that attitudes were forming round a hard core of theologians and directors; causing disruptive movements, and thereby needing to be suppressed" (p. 290). Louis's response was to exercise his

God-given right as sovereign. More often than not, repression became the order of the day.

Reacting to such movements, Louis revoked the Edict of Nantes in 1685. Enacted in 1598, the edict had been designed to give the Protestant Huguenots a form of recognition in Catholic France. As Catholicism had dominated France, the edict was viewed as a benevolent act toward the Huguenots.

A single-state religion was the norm for Europe's countries in those days. The issuance of such an edict had alarmed many who were used to the dictates of a reigning state church. While it was an obvious advantage for the Huguenots to have the edict, its provisions threatened those who demanded the status quo. When the revocation left a vacuum, Louis filled it with the Edict of Fontainebleau. This, of course, was a cleverly devised edict. It was specially formed to restrict Protestants even further by increasing the limitations placed upon the Huguenots.

When such crises occurred, Louis found the confines of Versailles refreshing. He spent lavishly on transforming what was once the Grand Chateau into a magnificent palace. His reputation as the Sun King was exemplified in his building of the Hall of Mirrors at Versailles. When visiting dignitaries came to see him, he would deliberately stand at the end of the hall, waiting until the sun was just right to reflect first upon the mirrors and then upon him. It was well known that departing ambassadors would report of their awe when returning home.

The need to maintain the grandeur of his name became paramount for Louis, known as "the Great." Louis worked feverishly at implementing technological advances within France, advances displayed in his palace at Versailles. Indeed, he became the first monarch known to have indoor plumbing within his quarters.

The legacy of Louis XIV could also be attributed to the fact that his reign was long. Louis was born in 1638 and died in 1715. He outlived his son, his grandson, and many who curried his favor during his life. His longevity was unusual for that day and age.

As a monarch, Louis XIV had both successes and failures. Many historians consider the Dutch War and the Revocation of the Edict of Nantes as blots on an otherwise positive and remarkable reign. Other wars were carried out for the glory of France. While they caused a drain on the treasury, the wars in which Louis XIV engaged left France in a far better position, leading to France's increased wealth and territory.

It is remarkable that Louis's legacy has persisted even to the present day. His legacy as the Sun King has remained intact. Versailles attracts thousands of visitors each year, with each visitor straining to absorb all that was the grandeur of Louis. His form of government proved efficient, and it would have remained if it had not been for the deadly upheaval of the French Revolution.

We are reminded of the passage of Scripture found in Mark 8:36 in the King James Version: "For what shall it profit a man, if he shall gain the whole world, and lose his soul?" Louis XIV built his legacy around both his persona and all that was France. It is a well-known fact that he had many vices as a man. Louis was known to have a rather voracious appetite, believed to be responsible in his later life for the onset of diabetes. The king favored many mistresses until he viewed them as having served their purpose. Their permanence would have clouded the issue of succession. Bernier states the following in *Louis XIV: A Royal Life*: "It has been given to few men not only to alter the course of history but also to create a myth which endures century after century" (p. 350). It is worth mentioning that Louis himself had hoped to perpetuate the myth as well.

By 1715 it had become clear that Louis XIV would not survive much longer. Preparations had been made, mostly by Louis himself, to continue the monarchy. It was a difficult challenge, as death had decimated the royal household. The duke d'Orleans, Louis's nephew, was charted as the next regent in line, as Louis's immediate successor, the dauphin, was only five years old at the time. Opposition from Louis's inner circle, however, had devised a plan to forestall the duke from taking power following the king's death. As Louis was prodded into placing it into his will, the duke became regent in name only.

We must interpolate a scenario that occurred prior to Louis's passing. It lends a humorous contrast to what we have known otherwise concerning Louis. Court records reflect that a charlatan had managed to pass through the gates of Versailles, claiming to be the shah of Persia. Courtiers and officials knew of his ruse but decided to introduce him to Louis in an elaborate setting. Louis was captivated that one from so far would come to see him at such an advanced age. Fitted in all of his fine regalia, he received the imposter at the other end of the great Hall of Mirrors. It is not known if he ever was informed of the visitor's true identity.

Louis's legacy can be viewed as superfluous. As king, he ranked the highest in grandeur among his peers. Here we must pose the question, "What about his soul?" On his deathbed, Louis XIV cried out, "O God, come to my help, please relieve me soon," notes Bernier (p. 348). From his last words, one may garner that, in the end, he felt that his soul was more important than his legacy.

2

The Legacy of David, Anointed King of Israel

We have seen the undertaking of Louis XIV, launched to perpetuate his enduring legacy. Louis XIV believed—indeed strove to remind both France and the world—that his anointing as king was a tangible, divine act attached permanently to his royal visage. The French validated that seal of anointing by virtue of his long and prosperous reign. Louis felt that he was divinely chosen, anointed by God alone to rule as king of France. One can argue that his legacy was still based upon all that he accomplished.

We will now see another king, one anointed not by people but by God to rule the kingdom of Israel. David's legacy is encapsulated by the biblical phrase, "a man after God's own heart." It endures as his legacy to both Israel and the generations of humanity. In order to examine this further, it is important to recognize that God validated David's anointing as king. David was the youngest of all his father's sons, and by society's standard, he was not suited to be the king of Israel.

We must therefore understand his anointing before we can accept his legacy.

Great kings receive anointing either by their people or, as in David's case, by God. In his book *Understanding the Anointing*, Kenneth E. Hagin states the following: "In the Old Testament, only the prophet, priest, and king were anointed" (p. 37). To show how the biblical practice of anointing relates to David, we must first view the definition and purpose of the words *anoint* and *anointing*.

In *Webster's Seventh New Collegiate Dictionary*, the word *anoint* is defined as "to designate as if through the rite of passage, anointment, or sacred consecration." Additionally, *Nelson's Illustrated Bible Dictionary* defines the words *anoint* and *anointing* as "to authorize, or set apart, a person for a particular work or service." According to this reference, King Louis and King David were both qualified, but their anointed missions were totally different from each other.

The anointed person belongs to God in a special sense. The phrases "the Lord's anointed," "God's anointed," "My anointed," or "His anointed" are used of Saul in 1 Samuel 26:9, 11, of David himself in 2 Samuel 22:51, and of Solomon in 2 Chronicles 6:42. More specifically, the *Ryrie Study Bible, New International Version* records the following in 2 Samuel 22:51 in reference to David: "He shows unfailing kindness to his anointed, to David and his descendants forever." This is a strong indicator of God's love specifically for His anointed. The same passage of Scripture also shows direct proof of God's own consecration and validation of David as "His anointed." It lends a greater foundation to David's legacy as a man after

God's own heart. Additionally, it sets apart the basis of the two legacies we have articulated thus far.

David is first mentioned in Scripture upon his anointing by the Lord through the prophet Samuel. Samuel had previously rejected all of Jesse's sons as candidates to be anointed. As mentioned in Scripture (1 Samuel 16:11), Jesse, David's father, mentioned that there was still one more son, the youngest, who was tending the sheep.

Jesse's answer revealed David as an unlikely candidate. His statement could also be seen as an indication that David still had work to do. David, certainly obeying the command of his father, came to Samuel and received the anointing of the Lord. We further find in 1 Samuel 16:12: "So he sent and had him brought in. He was ruddy with a fine appearance and handsome features. Then the Lord said, 'Rise and anoint him; he is the one.'" Verse 13 continues the scenario: "So Samuel took the horn of oil and anointed him in the presence of his brothers, and from that day on, the Spirit of the Lord came upon David in power" (*Ryrie Study Bible, NIV*). It is interesting to note that even the Spirit of the Lord made this anointing conclusive, as His own power rested upon David. We can therefore state that with the anointing of the Lord came power. Additionally, we can surmise that there was a divine transfer of power that came with the anointing of the Lord.

This anointing was the first of three for David. His second anointing came as king of Judah (2 Samuel 2:4) while his third was as king of all Israel (2 Samuel 5:3). In the presence of witnesses, his anointing became the binding authority needed to implement the Lord's plans and purposes. In turn, the fulfillment of the Lord's will through David's heart became his everlasting legacy.

There is a conveyance, an inescapable sense of God's presence in David's life as God directed him into his special destiny. David was more than aware of this, as it propelled him toward the greater purpose of fulfilling God's will. It is part of David's legacy that he desired to fulfill whatever God directed him to do.

In his book *Anointed to Reign*, Dr. Ronald Cottle submits the following: "The first major lesson, is the lesson of spiritual authority. David's very first act, after he caught a glimpse of his destiny, and felt the touch of God's anointing was to find a king to serve" (p. 6). David, aware of this fact, became a servant to King Saul. This is illustrated fully in 1 Samuel 16:21: "And David came to Saul, and stood before him: and loved him greatly; and he became Saul's armor bearer" (Ryrie). We now see David, a man on his way to fulfilling his destiny, anointed with power and a heart to serve. That same heart was challenged later when David faced events that would mold his hereditament.

Building upon David's recognition of God's anointing upon him, and his heart to serve, we must also factor in integrity. The word *integrity* comes from the root word *integer*. It literally means to be the same thing on the outside that one is on the inside. David's desire for integrity came from his sense of destiny, along with the power and anointing the Lord had already bestowed upon him. We can already see the solid layers that were beginning to form his future legacy.

When David projected himself into battle against Goliath, he not only had all odds against him, but he formed a confrontation of which legends are made. David provided a startling contrast to Goliath's elevated proportions. No other soldier in the army of Saul dared to confront such a giant. It was this battle that sparked his destiny. Armed with a mere sling, David was able to strike dead the colossal figure that had terrorized all of Israel. It marked the beginning of the journey that led him to his eventual rise as the king of Israel.

In Charles R. Swindoll's book *David: A Man of Passion and Destiny*, he makes a wonderful statement: "The beautiful thing about this story is that it's a perfect example of how God operates. He magnifies His name when we are weak" (p. 74). We see further, in David's defeat of Goliath, that the Lord's strength and anointing upon David enabled him to win the battle. Rather than relying upon Saul's armor or the surrounding army of Israel, David placed his trust in the Lord. His reliance was based upon what the Lord had already done for him in his life. It was the same reliance he would need again and again to fulfill his destiny and create his lasting legacy.

In F. B. Meyer's book *The Life of David,* he wrote the following: "Beloved of God and man, with a heart tremulous to the touch of love, the soil of David's soul was capable of bearing harvests to enrich the world. But his soul was also capable of the keenest suffering possible to man" (p. 25). David never hesitated in calling himself God's servant. Liable to hidden and presumptuous faults, David constantly thought of God as his rock. In fact, his recognition of God, as found in Scripture, served as a force that stabilized him throughout his life. It may be argued that his own identity as God's anointed servant allowed him to both endure and overcome the sufferings and trials he faced. It is noteworthy to mention that no legacy can be formed without such adversity. His anointing by the prophet Samuel was only the initial strengthening process. Adversity served to empower him further when he was later placed in a position of inheriting the throne of Israel.

Events in David's life—such as Saul's relentless pursuit of him to destroy his life, his recognition of failure after his fall with Bathsheba, and his anguish over Absalom—all pointed to a heart that cried out constantly for the Lord. This same heart is reflected in David's writing of the Psalms. David's character was constantly being shaped, molded, and etched by events both beyond and within his control. David did not always respond or react immediately to the situation at hand, while at other times he did. But it was always with a contrite heart that he sought resolution.

In his book *David, Seeking God Faithfully*, Gene A. Getz makes the observation: "It is easy to rationalize in our own hearts that another person cannot be trusted. We should review David's numerous attempts to trust Saul before he took his final course of action" (p. 123). Saul's pursuit of David, out of envy toward his successes, warranted swift judgment. David's response, however, again reflected God's character through his anointing. David responded with respect toward King Saul, recognizing him as God's servant and king, anointed by God as the first king of Israel. David's further legacy is his faith that God would deliver him, no matter what the circumstances at the time. His heart manifested God's position of trust in his life.

Whereas Louis the XIV inherited the throne of France, David's establishment on the throne of Israel was brought about chiefly by the crimes of his enemies and their destruction of each other as seen in 2 Samuel 3:8 and 4:8.

One does not see a tarnished legacy here. On the contrary, David was once again called "the Lord's anointed" as viewed in 2 Samuel 19:21 and 2 Samuel 23:1. As previously mentioned, we see a threefold anointing to kingship by Samuel (1 Samuel 16:11), by his own tribe Judah (2 Samuel 4:2), and by all of Israel (2 Samuel 5:2). God's Word confirms His selection and anointing upon David as Israel's king. In his book *All the Kings and Queens of the Bible*, Herbert Lockyer wrote the following passage: "The distinguishing peculiarity of David as a king was that he recognized in the most loyal manner, the higher loyalty to God, and regarded himself as a mere human vice-regent" (p. 110). It is noteworthy to state again that David's anointing opened his eyes to serving King Saul. Even as Israel's king, David sought to serve God as a servant. His legacy is once again prominently displayed through his humility and service to the Lord. David had the highest conception of his royal office, yet even at the height of his power, not once did he forget that he was God's instrument and servant.

It is extraordinary that David was the only king to be born in Bethlehem—save the King of King's, the very one he served. It was evidence of God's hand upon him. In Kenneth E. Hagin's book *A Fresh Anointing*, he comments, "It is the anointing of God which enables a person to stand in the office

God has called him to" (p. 7). It was also the anointing of God that enabled David to stand in his office as king. David was aware of this from the beginning, when the prophet Samuel placed him in front of his brothers and declared him to be God's choice as king.

In his book *Every Man in the Bible*, Larry Richards made the following statement: "The Old Testament prophets spoke of the coming of a promised Ruler, to spring from David's line that would fulfill the promise implicit in the historic reign of Israel's greatest King" (p. 44). Here, we see that David not only was anointed to rule as king but that from his lineage, Jesus, the Messiah, would also emerge, born also in Bethlehem as the King of Kings.

Many events in David's life directly connected the destinies of his personal life to that of Israel. In his book *Focus on the Bible, 2 Samuel, Out of Every Adversity*, Dale Ralph Davis stated, "King David's life meant the light of Israel; in one sense, David was Israel" (p. 229). The anointing placed upon David, and the legacy he created, spread across Israel, uniting the tribes and setting the stage for the glorious reign of his son Solomon.

David wanted to leave as his legacy the building of the temple for the Lord. His heart's desire was set upon creating the most magnificent structure ever erected for the God of Israel. The Word of God records that the sword of David prevented him from doing so. His kingdom had been at war for most of his reign. He ruled in Judah for seven years and in Israel for thirty-three—a total of forty years. His legacy remains: as the writer of the Psalms, a man after God's own heart, and the anointed King of Israel. David will also be remembered for his adulterous affair with Bathsheba and his departure from Jerusalem over the rebellion of his son Absalom. Regardless of his many faults, David's true legacy has been determined by his steadfast love of the Lord.

3

Esther, the Salvation of Her People

Out of the desert plateaus rises an unending cavalcade of barrenness. One would never think that such an impossible picture of abandonment and death would bear fruit of any kind. But when the rains fall, the desert blooms, and once again life appears unending. Such was the life of Hadassah (the Jewish name for Esther), orphaned and lowly, who rose up as the Queen of Persia "for such a time as this." Esther's legacy was engraved in history when she was willing to lay down her life for the salvation of her people.

Hadassah—that is, Esther—is first mentioned in Esther 2:7. Esther was an orphan. She was raised by her cousin Mordecai, whose uncle had been Esther's father. Mordecai raised Esther in the best of Jewish traditions, eventually taking her as his own daughter. We first find Esther in a setting of abandonment, much like a desert flower. She was unknown and ignorant of that which was about to be thrust upon her. A lovely young woman, she would soon rise to the highest position of any woman in the land.

The name Hadassah comes from the word *myrtle*. *Webster's New Collegiate Dictionary* defines the word *myrtle* as "any of a genus of shrubs, typifying a family of shrubs, including plants yielding spices." The myrtle is a plant of sweet scent and luxurious beauty. Like the myrtle, Hadassah bore the potential to become something great by virtue of the gifts she possessed. In the way that God looks at the heart, Esther more than qualified for greatness.

Just as the myrtle belongs to a family of shrubs that bear spices, Hadassah came from humble origins with the potential for greatness. She belonged to God's family and was chosen by Him as an instrument of deliverance.

Throughout the book of Esther, the name of God is noticeably absent. However, the hand of God, or the imprints of His presence, can be seen resting upon the life of Hadassah. When King Ahasuerus vanquished his former queen, Queen Vashti, a search was made for a suitable replacement regent.

As the king's commands and decrees were pronounced, young women throughout the kingdom were gathered in the capital city of Shushan. It was there, under the care of Hegai, the custodian of women, that Hadassah was taken to the king's palace.

The providential hand of God was clearly evident as Hadassah began her transformation as Esther. For an entire year, women throughout the kingdom of Persia were prepared in advance for presentation to King Ahasuerus. The lengthy process involved applications of makeup, oils, myrrh, and perfume. It is interesting to note that myrrh was representative of a preparation for holiness, brokenness, repentance, and a "dying to self." Incense was also applied during this period of time, symbolizing an attitude of worship, praise, and holiness. Esther's preparation reminds us of the preparation of Jesus' body for burial.

Whereas the name Hadassah meant "the myrtle," Esther, her new Persian name, meant "star." Certainly, a new star had appeared upon the horizon of her destiny.

After a year's worth of preparations, Esther was presented to King Ahasuerus. In Norman L. Geisler's book, *A Popular Survey of the Old Testament*, he wrote, "Esther found favor in the eyes of the King, above all other women" (p. 173). Undeniably beautiful, Esther had gained the absolute favor of the king. This would prove to benefit her as well as her people, for their time of need would soon arise. The considerable time devoted to Esther's preparation paid off handsomely when she was presented as the new queen of Persia. In the same way, a legacy takes time and patience to build. Nothing was done in vain. Likewise, Mordecai reaped the benefits of his close relationship to Esther, and he followed her to the palace.

We find that Esther's legacy began to unfold as Mordecai discovered an assassination plot against the king. Mordecai brought this information to Esther, who in turn warned the king. Esther understood her level of commitment and followed through. She recognized her position and, without hesitation, forged ahead in implementing her solution.

In the New King James Version of the Bible, we find Mordecai making a profound statement in Esther 4:14: "Who knows whether you have come to the kingdom for such a time as this?" Based on this statement alone, it can be said that Mordecai possessed great insight.

Through Esther's perseverance and determination, a situation that looked impossible transformed into one of hope. To approach the king required strength, humility, preparation, and commitment on her part. However, an even deeper level of commitment was needed when Haman, a court official, took offense toward Mordecai and somehow convinced the king to destroy the Jews.

Esther's sense of duty, calling, and service caused her to seek God's plan. Her loyalties were starkly divided between her husband and her people. When Mordecai pleaded with Esther to intervene, her true heart responded. She replied in anguish with a solution: "Gather all the Jews, fast and pray. If I perish, I perish." Her response was profound and heartfelt. Her legacy deepened and was imbedded in the minds of all people for all time.

Through these indicative actions, Esther displayed her character as a woman of God. Her virtues were demonstrated through prayer, fasting, wisdom, decisive action, and a willingness to lay down her own life. Esther did not allow the pomp, pageantry, or position to influence her heart away from God or her people. Her loyalty manifested brilliantly in a severe time of crisis. The positive attributes of her character proved flawless many times over. God's all-encompassing wisdom was revealed in that He alone knew how to match the individual character to the position for the occasion. God knew Esther's heart long before she became queen of Persia.

The *Illustrated Bible Dictionary, Volume I* denotes perhaps the only subtle negative portrayed in Esther's character. It states, "Although Esther was a brave woman, risking her life to save the Jews, the Bible does not commend her encouragement of the Jews to massacre their enemies in Chapter 9 of the book of Esther. Here, it can be said, she was a child of her age" (p. 478). This, ostensibly, could be seen as apathy toward revenge of her enemies or God's enemies.

In light of Esther's character, it may be argued that she was a type and shadow of Christ. She was willing to lay down her life. She recognized the right timing for entering the king's court and taking action. She allowed God to move through her, becoming an instrument of deliverance. As a result, God provided for the preservation of Esther's people, just as Christ became our provision. Additionally, Esther exhibited restraint and self-control at a turning point in history. She could have responded with fear, trepidation, and a flurry of emotions. Her reactions were pivotal in providing stability. It was obvious that God had anointed Esther with grace and favor. She was a recipient of His grace because of her humble status, and she won His favor by devotion and obedience.

In Charles R. Swindoll's book, *Esther: A Woman of Strength and Dignity*, he notes the following: "The great entrance into the throne room unannounced, is a defining point for Esther; indeed, her people" (p. 78). As Esther readied herself for her appearance before the king, all that she had learned—etiquette, presentation, humility, inner strength, dignity, and love of God—prepared her for a life-or-death decision.

Should the king's scepter fall, it meant sudden death. But if it were to rise, her life would be spared. This moment of unparalleled courage further distinguished her legacy. Esther displayed tact and courage, vital ingredients that formed the basis for deliverance.

Esther was granted favor by the king. She in turn requested a banquet. Her modesty and wit were revealed in her request, and up to half of the kingdom was hers for the asking. The evil Haman was outwitted by Esther's resolve and composure. He attended the banquet, pronounced judgment, and departed. The king granted Esther another request, whereupon she made an appeal to have her people spared and her adversaries judged accordingly.

Esther's methodical thinking was disclosed as all of her attributes came into play. Her selfless acts of intervention delivered her exiled nation and thus fulfilled her destiny. In honor of her legacy, her people established a celebration called Purim. It commemorates the day that the Jews battled their enemies for their lives, the day they were delivered from the massacre that Esther prevented. This historic day was first celebrated on the fourteenth day of Adar, which was the twelfth month of the Jewish year.

Although the bulk of her legacy would seem to exalt her status, and rightfully so, it is necessary to revisit the judgment that was meted upon her adversaries. With regard to Haman, who was wicked indeed, his sentence was inevitably predetermined. Haman was hanged on the very gallows he had designed for others. He deserved his fate.

Haman's ten sons shared the same doom, as did five hundred additional men killed in Shushan. But Esther evidently saw fit to carry out more retribution. When King Ahasuerus asked Esther if there was anything further he could do for her, Esther asked for another day in which the Jews could render justice. The request again was granted, with the result being that another several hundred were annihilated.

One might think that Esther went beyond the necessary reprisal to the point of being barbaric. She seemed determined to extinguish her enemies, once and for all. At the same time, we must ask ourselves, "Was not an entire race of people threatened with annihilation?" Would we have done the same as Esther? It is hard to imagine what actions would have been appropriate to the situation, as we were not there.

It is also important to recognize that regardless of what took place, Esther was God's agent. She was used for a specific purpose at a specific time in history. And while it remains true that Esther could have halted further judgment, history sees her divine legacy as one that saved her people from destruction. We are familiar with the passage of Scripture where the Lord says, "Vengeance is mine." Who is to say that Esther wasn't the vessel that carried out His will in His manner? Historians might consider this a negative attribute of Esther's character, but she served to fulfill her divine appointment. We are reminded in Scripture, "To do justice and judgment is more acceptable to the Lord than sacrifice" (Proverbs 21:3 KJV).

4

Last of the Romanov Dynasty

Much has been said and written about the Romanov Dynasty. It was, in and of itself, a family legacy that lasted over three hundred years. Begun in 1613 by its first Romanov czar, Mikhail Feodorovich, the Romanov family ruled the Russian Empire until its demise in 1917. With the abdication of its last czar, Nicholas II, a grand tradition of autocracy came to an end.

In its lineage, the Romanov Dynasty boasted such luminaries as Ivan the Terrible, Peter the Great, and Catherine the Great, Russia's truly illustrious woman empress. But it was the last vestige of the Romanov Dynasty that took power in 1894. In spite of all that had been accomplished throughout the preceding centuries—Peter the Great's modernization of Russia, for example—it was the family of Nicholas II and his rule that left a legacy entrenched in the minds of most. In part, this was due to the unfortunate events that surrounded him. But it was a barrage of bullets, ending with the death of the imperial family on July 17, 1918, that remained as the fateful epitaph and, hence, the Romanov legacy.

Several characters may come to mind when we think of Nicholas II: his wife, Alexandra; the Grand Duchesses Olga, Marie, and Tatiana; the legendary Anastasia, and the tsarevich Alexis. Beyond the family, others lurked behind the throne, whether invited or not. Vladimir Lenin, Joseph Stalin, and Alexander Kerensky were yet to appear on the stage of destruction.

One might also think of Rasputin, made famous in modern venues, or, again, Vladimir Lenin, who was chiefly responsible for the fall of the Romanov government and the subsequent murders of the royal family.

Nicholas Alexandrovich Romanov was born as heir to the Russian throne on May 18, 1868. The first of five surviving children of the czar, Alexander III, and his wife, the former Princess Dagmar of Denmark, Marie Fedorovna, Nicholas led a rather quiet and privileged childhood.

Nicholas was tutored by Constantine Pobedonostsev, who held the title of Procurator of the Holy Synod and was head of laity for the Russian Orthodox Church. His tutelage would leave an impact upon Nicholas, who sought the guidance and direction he would need for governing such a vast country. The Russian Orthodox Church, in essence, became the force behind the throne. In Peter Kurth's book, *The Lost World of Nicholas and Alexandra, Tsar*, he quotes a contemporary who wrote in his diary, "The Tsar is not God, but neither is he man. The Tsar is something between God and man" (p. 8). In Russia, the tsar (czar) was everything. It was a burden that Nicholas was more than well aware of. The institution of the church shaped his every thought and determined his every move.

As Nicholas's father was blessed with robust health, no one could have foreseen Nicholas's untimely death in 1894. Alexander III had saved his family in October of 1888 when the imperial train had derailed. His strength was enormous, as the czar had lifted the imploded roof, allowing the royal family to escape. His great feat had burnished his image as a man of tremendous might.

Advertisements and posters of the day had touted the "miracle of Borki" near the place where the train wreck had occurred. The anachronous demise of this towering figure in Nicholas's life would leave him ill-prepared for the throne. Indeed, Nicholas was preoccupied with matters other than ascending to his destiny. In *Nicholas and Alexandra*, author Robert K. Massie quotes Sergius Witte, Finance Minister of Russia, in a conversion with Nicholas's father, Alexander, in 1893: "Nevertheless, Sire, if you do not begin to initiate him to affairs of state, he will never understand them" (p. 24). The thought of preparing Nicholas for the throne was apparently not registering in Alexander's mind the year before his death. Undoubtedly, this would later explain Nicholas's propensity to retreat to private settings with his family when his life was fraught with the affairs of government. It was not a craving for privacy; rather it could be said that the affairs of state proved beyond his control.

Nicholas II ascended the throne of "Moscovy" upon the death of his father, Alexander III, on the twentieth of October in 1894. The death of Alexander caused the nation to shudder. It was an event that thrust Nicholas into a position he did not want. Duty compelled him to serve, and preparations were made accordingly. As it was customary for the events of ascension and coronation to take place separately, Nicholas took the crown of Russia in an elaborate coronation celebration a year and a half later in the spring of 1896. It was heralded as the event of the century.

The joyous occasion of the coronation could have marked a long and blissful reign. But Nicholas's circumstances and the events of his day would later control his destiny and eventual regrettable demise.

Dignitaries, nobility, and people of all walks of life gathered for the great event, including those at Khodynka Field, where over a million people had amassed to celebrate and welcome the new czar. Commemorative gifts had been readied, with Nicholas's portrait engraved on cups, mugs, plates, and everything imaginable. The distribution of these valuable items, along with the prospect of viewing the newly anointed monarch, brought more people than the authorities had anticipated. Khodynka Field had been used as a military training field and was dotted with abandoned wells, wide ditches, and various gullies. Emergency preparations were nonexistent, as was the oversight needed to avert any unforeseen calamity.

People arrived by the thousands and decided to stay through the night to ensure their place at the front of the festivities for the following day. As darkness fell, thousands more arrived and surged forward, causing many to be trampled to death. The date would come to be known as Bloody Saturday. This particular event, the first ill-fated one of his reign, would place Nicholas in an untenable position.

Festivities had been paid for, and thousands of notable guests had arrived to join in the revelry. His dilemma caused him to consider the delay of auxiliary celebrations, but it was to his detriment that he did not. We must consider in hindsight that it unhinged his rule from the beginning.

Upon further examination of this disastrous episode, we find an explanation as to the new moniker that Nicholas would inherit. Nicholas obviously had to have felt anguish and distress over the loss of so many of his adoring subjects. However, it was his view that, ostensibly, the show must carry on. Concerts continued and performances remained on schedule at the Bolshoi Theatre. Balls, banquets, military parades, and all that had been planned continued as though nothing had happened.

The damage now done, Nicholas issued his royal manifesto, which contained his assertion of an unbroken bond between the czar and his subjects. It further stated that he would serve for the good of Russia. It would prove to be an inauspicious start, an ominous sign of things to come, for public opinion had already turned sour. Indeed, it was altogether negative.

The emperor was now openly stigmatized for not conforming to propriety. Although Nicholas and his family attended to the injured at hospitals, and even made their presence known at requiem services, his reputation would be marred throughout his tenure. No good work could undo the impression left upon the populace. Even those close to the throne held similar opinions. Over ninety thousand rubles were raised by the nobility for the victims, but the negative perception remained. Nicholas II, from this time forward, became known as Nicholas the Bloody, or Bloody Nicholas. Events would prove beyond his control. It was truly the first brick laid in the foundation of an unfortunate legacy for both Nicholas and the dynasty.

The epithet applied to him was neither accurate nor fair. Peter the Great, though known as "the Great," impaled the heads of rebellious Cossacks upon spiked chariot wheels throughout Moscow. But Nicholas, a true adherent of the Russian Orthodox Church, possessed the overriding qualities of compassion and virtue. The negative appellation assigned to his image and person would scar his family, his rule as czar, and all attempts made at future reform.

It is worth mentioning again that it was on the seventeenth of October that Alexander III saved his family from the train derailment at Borki. That same date was declared as "October Day," or "Revolutionary Day," in old Soviet times when the Bolsheviks of Vladimir Lenin took over in 1917. Whether it was an intentional act of vengeance or a deliberate defacing of the Romanov family by Lenin and his followers, it nevertheless served as a date of importance. Ironically, it also marked the day when Nicholas II signed a limited manifesto of reform in 1905. Although it was filled with good intentions, the nature of the Russian autocrat would inevitably restrict its usage, as Nicholas II was a man of contradictions. He was torn between preserving the birthright and heritage that "God and Russia had accorded him," and moving further ahead with reforms that would take Russia well into the twentieth century.

It is speculation on our part to conclude that Nicholas had a fear of the unknown, but his own diary has provided some supplementary insight as to his reasoning. *The Sunset of the Romanov Dynasty*, written by Mikhail Iroshnikov, Liudmila Protsai, and Yuri Shelayev, records Nicholas's diary entry: "17ᵗʰ October, Monday, Anniversary of the accident ... signed the manifesto ... my head has grown heavy, my thoughts confused. O Lord, help us to pacify Russia" (p. 16). It was the source of his contradictions that further molded the legacy of the House of Romanov.

There was, however, a bright spot in the House of Romanov. The previous year of 1904 had seen the birth of the Tsarevich Alexis. It was a joyous occasion, as it heralded the arrival of the heir to the Russian throne. But another adverse element in the legacy of the Romanov family had yet to be revealed. After his birth, Alexis bled profusely at his navel. It was soon discovered that he had inherited hemophilia from his great-grandmother, Queen Victoria. Episodes of bleeding would occur throughout Alexis' short life. It dominated the focus and attention of the imperial family. It would open the door to the likes of spiritualists and charlatans who sought the favor of Nicholas and Alexandra.

We have, thus far, focused on Nicholas II, and rightfully so. It was Nicholas who carried the image and ultimate legacy of the House of Romanov. But it was his wife, Alexandra Feodorovna, who bore the brunt of the possibility that Alexi could die at any time. It is unfortunate that many books and publications have painted a picture of Alexandra as an uncaring mother or dominant figure in running Russia while Nicholas was at the front during World War I.

While it is true that Alexandra suffered great bouts of depression, this should not be considered her legacy. Alexandra's mind was consumed with the daily well-being of her son. If he had a good day, her mood reflected it. If his health took a turn for the worse, her will to live waned precariously.

Even Alexandra's personal physician, Dr. Yevgeny Botkin, considered the empress "not quite normal." Her psychological condition was certainly a preoccupation of his, just as Alexis' health was to her. Her treatment in this case was probably lacking or nonexistent. We do not know what Nicholas thought, but his response to his wife was always impeccable. The royal family, being secretive out of necessity, placed themselves in a position of guarding their privacy, particularly where Alexis was concerned. Alexandra relentlessly sought for a miracle for Alexis, turning toward whatever gave her the greatest hope.

Nicholas and Alexandra were deeply religious and devout adherents to the Russian Orthodox Church. Their sincerity and devotion were displayed at government events as well as major calendar holidays. Iconography was prominently displayed. The Seraphim of Sarov, a monk known for his miraculous attributes, was of particular interest to the royal couple. His icon and noted ability to help women suffering from infertility was of keen interest to Alexandra. Nicholas and Alexandra, in fact, celebrated a service lasting several hours that was dedicated to his memory. In the following year, 1904, both of them credited that same service with Alexandra's giving birth to the heir to the throne.

In retrospect, it seems doubtful that Nicholas and Alexandra had a full knowledge of the Word of God, as most of their actions and responses were based upon traditional aspects of the church in Russia. Nevertheless, their sincerity and devotion toward pleasing God must be seen as applying their utmost in fulfilling His will. This would later explain their reliance upon the likes of Rasputin. It brings to mind a passage of Scripture found in Matthew 15:16 (KJV) where Jesus said, "Are ye also yet without understanding?" It could be argued that Nicholas and Alexandra certainly had hearts for God but lacked understanding.

Other than the birth of the tsarevich, 1904 and 1905 would prove inimical to the dynasty. Nicholas II had grand illusions of expanding the boundaries of the Russian Empire. The Russo-Japanese War had started when the Japanese had launched an attack against Russia, causing damage to several warships at Port Arthur. Although justified in retaliating, Nicholas was relegated to defeat when an armistice was signed. It was the beginning of a ripple effect that would eventually cause his abdication years later.

Nicholas's government became even more tremulous upon the events of January 9, 1905. On that day, thousands of workers gathered at the Winter Palace to petition Nicholas and present their grievances. Nicholas, who knew of the upcoming march, had left the area out of vigilance. Cossacks fired upon the crowd, and thousands died. It became known as "Bloody Sunday." "Bloody Nicholas" was held responsible for Bloody Sunday.

Public reaction was swift and immediate, as underground pamphlets were distributed denouncing the government and the czar. Foreign governments withheld financial obligations to Nicholas, causing further stress upon the treasury. Nicholas himself expressed "forgiveness towards his subjects" for walking into inevitable consequences. This would provide a further stain upon his legacy. It could be said that it was here that the seeds of revolution were born.

Strikes and further upheavals placed Nicholas in the untenable position of making choices constantly. His predecessors had not had to face what he did, and Russia was unraveling around him. Nicholas reacted with indecisiveness and contradiction. He signed a manifesto creating the State Duma. One year later, on the anniversary of Bloody Sunday in January of 1906, he dissolved it. From the time of the first State Duma until the last in 1917, Nicholas II vacillated between granting more privileges and increasing the authority inheritably found in autocracy.

The nobility of Russia, and Nicholas himself, responded characteristically—by marking notable anniversaries with festivals and grand balls. It was at such an event that Grigori Rasputin first came into prominence with Nicholas and, in particular, Alexandra. Rasputin, a *starets*, or holy man, was introduced to the emperor and empress through those who were aware of his ability to cure diseases, sicknesses, and all forms of maladies. His reputation as such preceded him wherever he traveled. Rasputin's introduction to the court of Romanov transformed history forever.

It is a notable fact and enduring mystery that Rasputin possessed a detailed knowledge of the disease hemophilia. In Alexandra's eyes, she had found the cure for her son Alexis. Rasputin's undue influence upon the imperial family would eventually take its toll, as the royal family did nothing without consulting him. Inevitably, Rasputin was called whenever Alexis was found bleeding. There are recorded incidents of Rasputin having prayed or made the sign of the cross, whereby Alexis was healed and ceased to bleed. One might speculate that the royal family's strong belief in Rasputin's ability to heal caused them to place their faith and trust in him rather than in God.

An interesting aspect of Rasputin's own legacy is found in his belief that "one should sin more, in order that one's salvation is the greater." History shows that this core doctrine would further corrupt the nobility and those in high society. It would further increase the fragility of Mother Russia, taking her to the point of no return.

The year of 1913 could be considered the apogee of the House of Romanov for Nicholas II and his family. No one could have foretold that within five years, his family would be murdered, and the monarchy replaced by revolutionaries. The year 1913 was celebrated all throughout Russia, as the populace recognized three hundred years of Romanov rule. Nobility and peasants alike reveled in feasts, dances, festivals, and marches, from Moscow to Siberia. They paraded icons of Nicholas and his family. The grain harvests of that year were exceptional, allowing Nicholas's subjects a rare surplus.

It appeared as if all past ominous events would be forgotten, facilitating the dawn of a new age. Some dared to believe that a constitutional monarchy was in order. Even the usually turbulent reactionaries were quieted, as Lenin had placed his subversive activities on hold. The monarchy was strengthened, and the people were generally happy. This would herald, in the following year, an apocalypse never to be forgotten.

The events of World War I changed the landscape, not only of Russia but of every throne and royal household in Europe. Russians initially supported the czar's entry into the war, as the honor of Russia was at stake. The eventual mounting of casualties, however, changed support into open hostility. Riots became commonplace as people sought food for their families. Taxation and the burden it produced took its toll.

While all appeared to unravel in the capital, Nicholas attended to military matters at the front, apparently oblivious to the gravity of the crisis. His appearance and that of the tsarevich, Alexis, energized his soldiers for the defense of the country. It provided for Nicholas a release from ordinary governmental affairs. Alexandra had been left in St. Petersburg to manage the affairs of state by proxy. Her own tenuous position caused her to rely increasingly upon Rasputin for divine guidance. Forces were arrayed against Rasputin as well as the monarchy. The clouds of adversity appeared to gather at frightening speed. It would only be a matter of time before sudden destruction would strike the Russian Empire and the imperial family itself.

We are again reminded of the magnitude of events as pronounced in Scripture: "Now gather thyself in troops, O daughter of troops: he hath laid siege against us" (Micah 5:1 KJV). Nicholas and Alexandra seemed oblivious to the chaos that had encircled them.

Many saw Rasputin as the evil instigator, the one responsible for military carnage and the many problems that faced the nation. He had mostly critics and detractors, but his staunchest ally was found in Alexandra. Her protection, however, was not impervious. A plot had been hatched for Rasputin's demise. His death left history open to speculation.

Perhaps it was Rasputin's own legacy to determine that of the House of Romanov. We can find ourselves enraptured at the thought of what might have been if Grigori Rasputin had not walked into the lives of Nicholas and Alexandra. We are often fascinated with the hindsight of history and the prospect of what may lie ahead or what might have been. Rasputin, nevertheless, impacted the legacy of the Romanov Dynasty by his direct manipulation of Alexandra. In turn, her influence impacted Nicholas II. It was a perpetually revolving door. Others recognized this fact and took matters into their own hands.

The princes of Romanov viewed Rasputin as a charlatan and a madman. Through an invitation to a party, devised by assailants, Rasputin was finally murdered. Legend has it that he was stabbed, shot, and finally drowned—only to come back to life. His body was found in a frozen river.

His death caused Nicholas to banish Prince Yusupov, one of the perpetrators, to his estate in the south of Russia. It was a move that spared the prince's life during the upheaval that was to follow. Alexandra went into further depression, for she felt that her connection to God now ceased to exist.

Shortly before his murder, Rasputin wrote somewhat prophetically regarding Russia's future. He stated that "if he died a natural death, then Russia would be spared, along with the monarchy ... if not, both would perish." Such writings are for speculation and not for evidence of a true prophet. Additionally, the source of this quote has not been noted, as its authenticity has not been verified. However, it escalates the legend and legacy of Grigori Rasputin.

By 1917, World War I had been raging for over two years or more. Devoid of the life it had once known, Russia was beginning to convulse more frequently. Unemployment was ever higher, while food reserves became critically low. Anti-government rallies were more and more common. Alexandra and her daughters worked for the war effort. Volunteering their services at hospitals provided great relief for them as well as the soldiers they attended. As events worsened, Nicholas was suddenly faced with the prospect of abdication. Pressured from all sides, and for the good of Russia, he relented, albeit unwillingly. After this traumatic episode in his life, many contemporaries of the day noted his demeanor improving. Nicholas now felt free to concentrate on his family and the simpler life he had so longed for.

A provisional government was set in place prior to the abdication. Even with concessions, the state of affairs proved tenuous at best. The gravity of the situation was further reflected in a telegram sent to Nicholas at the front lines of the war. In *The Sunset of the Romanov Dynasty*, the authors record the following from one of Nicholas's ministers: "The hour that will decide your fate and that of our homeland has struck. Tomorrow may already be too late" (p. 187). It was part of Nicholas's legacy that he responded with apathy. This would prove to be another nail in the dynasty's coffin.

Alexander Kerensky served as chairman of the provisional government in 1917, but even his position was unsecured. The volatile atmosphere of the day served to remind anyone in power that anything could happen at any time. Events had severely curtailed the efforts of any government that wished to serve at that time.

Without a doubt, the very monarchy itself had been threatened with extinction. Nicholas had abdicated in favor of his brother, Grand Duke Mikhail. Mikhail had acknowledged this position and responded only on the condition that free elections would be held and respect given to the State Duma. He faced an impossible task. It was inevitable that he too would soon renounce the throne. This would herald the end of more than three hundred years of autocratic rule by the House of Romanov. It is easy to question how matters spiraled out of control. We are reminded once again of Khodynka Field and Bloody Saturday.

The legacy of Nicholas II, his family, and the Romanov Dynasty would not be complete without telling of the horrific murders that annihilated his family. This one major episode has lodged itself in the minds of millions around the world, spawning tales regarding the fate of Nicholas's daughter Anastasia. Human nature generally hopes for survivors in any case. It is important, therefore, to give an account of the events that led to their imprisonment and subsequent execution.

Nicholas was fatalistic regarding the future. He was quoted in the memoirs of a contemporary as such. *The Sunset of the Romanov Dynasty* says, "I sense with a firm and absolute certainty that the fate of Russia, my own fate, and the fate of my family are in the hand of God" (p. 337). In 1917 Nicholas could not have foreseen that he and his family had little time left to their lives.

The Petrograd government of Vladimir Lenin had ordered the family of the czar to be placed under house arrest at the Alexander Palace for five months' time. The crowned heads of Europe, though related to Nicholas II, wanted nothing to do with the debased emperor. Even George V of Britain, whom many considered an exact likeness of Nicholas himself, did not lend his support.

Revolutionary passions in the wartime capital of Petrograd forced the provisional government of Alexander Kerensky to exile the royal family to Siberia. Nicholas and his family, along with what remained of their retinue, lived in relative tranquility for the remainder of 1917 and into the first half of 1918.

The provisional government of Alexander Kerensky fell even faster than that of the czar. Vladimir Lenin seized power, recognizing that the war with Germany would impede any further success. Peace was eventually implemented, but it exacted a terrible price. Lands that had been in the hands of Russia for centuries were ceded to the German empire. Nicholas received the news with great bitterness. Although we may never know, we must think that at that point, Nicholas may have regretted his abdication.

It is reasonable to surmise that at some point Vladimir Lenin made a decision to put Nicholas and his entire entourage to death. The new Soviet administration was virulently anti-monarchy. Those who wished for a public trial for Nicholas, his family, radicals, and subversives demanded its implementation. Plans were set into motion for a transfer, ostensibly for trial in Moscow. En route to their destination and destiny, the train carrying the imperial family was halted, disarmed, and redirected. Several months of calm in Siberia had provided a false sense of security in the minds of the royal family, who remained unsuspecting. We are reminded of Nicholas's faith in God that their lives were in His hands. Surely their reliance upon Him had intensified. We must ask ourselves: did they rely upon their knowledge of salvation during this time?

In spite of genuine orders from Moscow to bring the family to trial, we must conclude that while they were in transit, Lenin had implemented his own devices. Who else would have had the authority to seize the imperial family? It was a journey wherein the unforeseen would occur.

Nicholas and his family had presented a real and impending danger to the new Soviet command. As a result, they were taken to Ekaterinberg, the fiercest center of Bolshevism in all of Russia. It was here that the legacy of Nicholas II, his family, and the last of the Romanov Dynasty grew to legendary proportions. The narrative of their execution has remained a fixation for almost one hundred years. Referring to Robert K. Massie's book, *Nicholas and Alexandra*, we find a chilling quote from Jacob Yurovsky, the chief assassin of the Romanov family and their attendants: "Tonight, we will shoot the whole family, everybody. Notify the guards outside not to be alarmed if they hear shots" (p. 516).

The massacre of the czar and his family has survived as a legend full of mystery and tragedy. The family was kept under virtual arrest at the Ipatiev house in Ekaterinberg. They spent their time conducting services and prayers while living on what was provided for them. On the night of July 17, 1918, the family was awakened and told that they would be leaving. Jacob Yurovsky himself led them into the basement, and they gathered in chairs to await their next destination. The plan for their execution had been vigilantly concealed.

Everyone in the imperial entourage assembled in silence. We know that those who gathered on that dreadful night included Nicholas, Alexandra, their four daughters, and the heir Alexis; their personal physician, Dr. Botkin; their chef, Kharitonov; a valet by the name of Trupp; and Demidova, Alexandra's personal maid. It is important to mention all eleven, as later events would contribute to both the legacy and mystery that followed.

It was Yurovsky who first reentered the basement, along with his execution squad, after all eleven had come together. In Robert K. Massie's book, *Nicholas and Alexandra*, Yurovsky's last words to the royal family and attendants are recorded: "Your relations have tried to save you. They have failed, and we must now shoot you" (p. 517). At this point, the legendary mystery would take root.

Nicholas rose from his chair in vain, attempting to protect his family. He was immediately shot dead. Alexandra reacted with the sign of the cross, faithful to the very end in her devotion to God. She died when struck by a single bullet. Three of the czar's daughters—Marie, Olga, and Tatiana—also died in the salvo of ammunition. The physician, chef, and valet followed. Alexandra's maid, Demidova lived through the hail of bullets, only to succumb to bayonets. Alexis and Anastasia also survived the initial barrage, but they too were stilled.

From this point forward, all that has been said or written must be considered speculation. Varying accounts have been offered that Anastasia and Alexis survived. Others contended that their bodies were burned in acid and buried in a forest outside present day Yekaterinburg alongside members of their family and servants. In past decades, many people have come forward, claiming to be either the tsarevich or Anastasia. The possible survival of Anastasia has launched movies, books, and theatrical productions worldwide. One woman by the name of Anna Anderson claimed that she was the surviving grand duchess, Anastasia. Her story has fascinated numerous people for years.

It is evident that Nicholas II and Alexandra wished to leave a radiant legacy for the Russia they dearly loved. It is a regrettable epitaph that other events marred that quixotic view. We must ask ourselves, therefore, what could have changed the outcome of such a legacy? We must again take a look at the beginning of events that first unfolded after the coronation of Nicholas II.

What if Nicholas had canceled celebrations immediately after the catastrophe of Khodynka Field? Regardless of his later attending services and numerous Orthodox masses commemorating the tragedy, would the immediate cessation of festivities have endeared Nicholas to the Russian populace? Is it possible that such an action would have altered the perception that Nicholas was indifferent or tyrannical? Considering the manifesto of 1905, what if Nicholas's character had been free of indecisiveness or inconsistency? Would he have left the fledging State Duma intact? Would this have left Russia in a far better position, placing it on the narrow path toward a constitutional monarchy?

Regarding the events of Bloody Sunday in 1905, what if Nicholas's contingent of Cossacks in charge had not of fired upon the masses of peasants marching to see the czar? What if Nicholas had visited them himself? Would that have changed his legacy? We must recognize that hindsight always has the advantage over foresight. We cannot possibly know his every thought. We can, however, remind ourselves that Nicholas once stated, "I never had another thought than to serve the country which God had entrusted me" (*The Sunset of the Romanov Dynasty*, 337).

5

The Legacy of Martin Luther King Jr.

Thus far, we have seen how people's characteristics have led to either their detriment or advantage. Those who possessed more than just a mere knowledge of God, such as King David and Esther, overcame the adversities that faced them. Their deeper understanding of God placed them at a greater advantage for the future.

Others, such as Louis XIV and Nicholas II, remained true to their traditions of God. They acknowledged Him as their superior, but they may have lacked the perception of what it meant to have a relationship with their Creator. While Louis XIV may have used his Catholicism as a repository for his actions, Nicholas II reverted to his Russian Orthodoxy as a sanctuary from obligations that confronted him daily. It could be said that these approaches led to their detriments and defined their legacies accordingly.

Martin Luther King Jr. formed a legacy that is perceived as an explicit advantage for humanity. An American clergyman and civil rights leader, Dr. King was born in 1929 in Atlanta,

Georgia, the son of Martin Luther King Sr. and Alberta King. King left a distinct legacy through his support for civil rights, demonstrating an understanding of and passionate love for God. It was to his benefit, and that of humanity, that he led black Americans toward establishing such rights. His achievement in the field of civil rights has been recognized and celebrated throughout the world. It could be argued that his unwavering support of the disadvantaged would later cost him his life in April of 1968.

Martin Luther King Jr. was the son of Reverend Martin Luther King Sr., the pastor of Ebenezer Baptist Church. Martin's original name was Michael King, which was changed to Martin Luther King Jr. when he was five. It is believed that his name change was a reflection of his family's admiration for Martin Luther, the Protestant reformer who was born in the 1500s. King himself would later become the minister of the Dexter Avenue Baptist Church in 1954 in Montgomery, Alabama. The strong foundational support that his father and family provided for him was reflected in his passionate faith in God. Martin knew that "he could do all things through Christ who strengthened him." Martin's legacy was grounded in God.

King's early impression of segregation, where white and black children were sent to separate schools, left a prevailing feeling upon him. King's best friends were white children. As friends, they attended different schools. His initial response was quoted in Michael Schuman's book, *Martin Luther King Jr., Leader for Civil Rights*: "I still didn't think much about it at first. But suddenly when I would run across the street after school to compare notes, their mother would tell them that they could not play (with me) anymore" (p. 17). Martin's mother would later explain to him that prejudice came from fear.

Martin was influenced by his father's emotional reaction to racism. Martin had been with his father when they were told to stand at the back of the store when purchasing a pair of shoes. His father, more than once, had expressed his opposition, vowing to oppose unfair laws and practices to his death. This would later be an underlying factor in creating Martin's legacy.

Martin Luther King Jr. was counted among a group of intelligent young men selected to attend Morehouse College in 1944. Martin was only fifteen when he entered. Prior to graduation, King received an award for a composition and speaking contest. His theme was entitled "The Negro and the Constitution." It proved to be the first of many speeches that he would deliver later. King was also influenced by two professors at Morehouse College: Dr. Benjamin Mays and George Kelsey. Each would lay a foundation in Martin's life, establishing the rights of education and the basis of religious beliefs. Both stressed to King the importance of ministers confronting societal problems.

King later joined an organization called the Intercollegiate Council. Made up of white and black students, it served as an important instrument in forming his attitudes about race relations. Its members were sympathetic to the struggles that many black Americans faced, thereby lessening any negative preconceptions that King may have formed.

Martin Luther King Jr. attended Crozer Theological Seminary, earning a degree in divinity in 1951. It was while at Crozer that King heard Dr. Mordecai Johnson speak on protesting against unjust laws. His method espoused that of Mahatma Gandhi in India: civil disobedience through peaceful methods. Gandhi had formed techniques for resisting the British government's rule over India. When Indians were beaten, Gandhi taught passive resistance by calling on those affected to endure the hardship of such punishment.

Dr. Johnson was to further Martin Luther King's vision of creating equal rights for all. King was impacted by Dr. Johnson's approach and Gandhi's process. They would form the basis for his enacting civil rights throughout the United States. In Marshall Frady's book, *Martin Luther King Jr.*, he illustrates this point with an observation made in later years: "King would in fact, aside from the constant shadow of bomb and assassination threats, be personally attacked a number of times over the years" (p. 51). We are reminded of Luke 6:29 (KJV): "And unto him that smiteth thee on the one cheek offer also the other." It was a credit to King's legacy that his methods were acquired early in his fight for civil rights.

Martin Luther King Jr. served as an associate pastor at his father's church in Atlanta. This position provided valuable experience in speaking before large crowds. He later enrolled in Boston University during the same year. Two professors who taught there, Dr. Edgar Sheffield and Harold DeWolf, helped to form King's philosophy that the true God was a personal one, and that every human being had dignity and worth.

King believed that everyone was worthy of redemption if he could accept God's love and mercy. He earned his Doctorate of Philosophy in 1955.

Martin Luther King Jr. was married to Coretta Scott on June 18, 1953. Her support during the struggle for civil rights would prove invaluable. Following their marriage, Martin took a position as pastor at the Dexter Baptist Church in 1954 in Montgomery, Alabama. Martin and Coretta had four children.

The year 1954 would further define the life and legacy of Martin Luther King Jr. The Supreme Court had weighed in on a major decision in the case of *Brown v. Board of Education of Topeka*. In it, the court overruled the idea of "separate but equal" as it pertained to the public school systems within the United States. Segregation was dealt a major defeat. Schools throughout the country, and the south in particular, were opposed to any changes that would infringe on their way of life. It was this decision that galvanized black Americans to fight further for rights that were inherently theirs.

The embryonic stages of civil disobedience began with Martin Luther King Jr. at the front. King was selected as an activist and spokesman for the Montgomery Improvement Association, an organization formed around the Montgomery bus boycott. The boycott had been formed after Rosa Parks refused to surrender her bus seat to white patrons. It was a citywide boycott that would last for over a year. It ended when the Supreme Court rejected the City of Montgomery's bus segregation laws. The process was not entirely peaceful, as the homes of King and other supporters had been bombed.

King organized the Southern Christian Leadership Conference, which gave him a base to pursue further civil rights activities. Established first within the southern states, it later grew to become nationwide. The SCLC worked toward the registration of millions of black American voters. It was during this time of campaigning for registration that Martin wrote his first book, *Stride Toward Freedom*, which was published in 1958.

On June 23, 1958, Martin Luther King Jr. met with President Eisenhower concerning the implementation of the first Civil Rights Act passed in 1957. King's national prominence was at the forefront and earned him the cover of *Time Magazine* in 1957. King continued his nonviolent approach to civil disobedience, participating in sit-ins that were held across the country.

In Vincent P. Franklin's book, *Martin Luther King Jr.*, he records the historic event of King's further involvement in the Civil Rights movement: "King issued the 'Birmingham Manifesto,' which called for the desegregation of all lunch counters, department stores, rest rooms, and drinking fountains in downtown department and variety stores" (p. 85). It was this issuance that ignited the March on Washington in August of 1963. That year, thousands would gather together to hear King's famous "I Have a Dream" speech.

Opposition to King's actions and policies were felt at every level. City and government officials employed tactics of every kind to prevent King's movement from advancing forward. Opposition even rose from southern churches that were predominately white at the time. We are reminded of

King's foundational belief that God had his hand upon him. In Frank Damazio's book, *The Making of a Leader*, he states, "Most Christians believe that God guides his people. But many do not believe that He uses the leaders who are walking with Him, to do so" (p. 251). Opposition even commenced from the black community; some thought that King was moving too fast, while others thought he was not moving fast enough.

Martin Luther King's philosophy of nonviolent resistance led to his arrest on numerous occasions. On one such occasion, King was arrested in Montgomery. A photographer captured the moment, featuring King's face across national papers on the following morning. King appeared on the same day for an interview on NBC's *Today* show. It was later that afternoon, while signing copies of his book, that a deranged woman stabbed him in the chest. King's reaction was characteristic of him; he asked that she be taken to a hospital for help.

When remembering Martin Luther King Jr., one is reminded of the March on Washington. Launched on August of 1963, more than two hundred and fifty thousand people— black, white, and all races—joined together to listen to Martin Luther King's "I Have a Dream" speech. In it, he emphasized unity and the equality of all men. King's momentous speech at the Lincoln Memorial would forever be remembered. It would be the defining moment of his brief legacy, capturing for all time he was all about.

Martin Luther King Jr. was further recognized in 1963 when he was selected as *Time Magazine*'s "Man of the Year" and was referred to as "the symbol of the Negro Revolution." The following year would continue King's legacy, as the 1964

Civil Rights Act was passed by Congress and signed into law by President Lyndon Johnson. It was a crowning achievement that would probably have been long delayed without the help of Martin Luther King Jr. In 1964 King was also awarded the Nobel Peace Prize. It was recognition justly deserved, as King had fought nonviolently for civil rights.

King's leadership in the Civil Rights Movement was challenged in the 1960s. His interests, however, widened from civil rights to include criticism of political corruption, and concern over poverty. He spearheaded several actions on poverty reforms, religion, and rights for the disabled.

Martin Luther King was a powerful and eloquent speaker, as well as author. In addition to what we have already mentioned, King wrote, "Why We Can't Wait" in 1964, and "Where Do We Go from Here: Chaos or Community?" in 1967.

Martin Luther King's vision was of a cooperative, unified society. Some would call it a reconciling of King's dream with reality, a more practical approach to positive change in any community. The differences in society during Martin Luther King's time were deemed insurmountable. His was a positive and hopeful message, one that would resonate long after his death.

Martin Luther King championed tolerance and respect for life. One could say that tolerance has no cohesive healing power in society. Indeed, there is a relative sense in tolerance that leads to indifference and not understanding. It could be viewed as a weak point in Martin Luther King's crusade for civil rights. It must be noted, however, that King was not advocating tolerance. His thunderous desire was to lodge in people the idea of love. The love that Martin Luther King possessed was based upon God's love for him. That same love caused him to have no fear, or his legacy was such that he did not show it. In Martin Luther King's own book, *Strength to Love*, he wrote the following: "Hate cannot drive out hate, and only love can do that" (p. 51).

It is probable, almost certain, that King knew the Scriptures better than most. We are reminded of one passage that reflected upon him well: "Herein is our love made perfect, that we may have boldness in the day of judgment: because as He is, so are we in this world" (1 John 4:17 KJV). King was able to act with boldness, as he believed that God would bless his efforts. With King's boldness toward enacting civil rights reform, the ingredient of fearlessness had to be present. We are again reminded of Scripture in 1 John 4:18 (KJV): "There is no fear in love; but perfect love casteth out fear." Having no fear, with God's boldness, Martin Luther King was able to achieve what most have only dreamed of: a legacy to benefit all of humanity.

As we consider giving life to King's dream, we must acknowledge that in his speaking and writing, that dream begins with God. Without God there is no absolute truth on which to base a call to justice. Nor is there any other source from which to draw strength to exhibit the love of which he spoke. It was King's vision to be an instrument in imparting justice through God's love.

Too often, those who claim to be Christians have failed to live in keeping with the clear teachings of Christian Scripture. It has been stated clearly in the Bible (and Dr.

King affirmed) that the church ought to provide spiritual and moral leadership in society. However, as we observe the history of American churches, we see that many of them have been passive or even regressive in matters of individual or societal differences.

Martin Luther King's legacy was grounded in God. One might consider that without this divine anointing, this calling upon Reverend King's life, there would be no reform. Segregation and the unlawful racial abuse of people would still be existent in our times. In becoming obedient to his calling, King had to overcome not only the difficulties of his day but the war that was waging within him. By a powerful divine decree, he became the voice of many ideals and a force to be reckoned with.

Dr. King's life was devoted to challenging his nation to living out a more consistent obedience to the moral absolutes of the Bible. Some sermons he gave were reported pleas for men and women to enter into the kind of personal relationship with God that he treasured, one that transcended what could be seen and was currently being experienced.

It might have been easier for any individual to adopt a more peaceful life, if such a life could have been possible for a black clergyman of his time. We have recognized the sacrifices that Dr. King brought into our society. His ideas inspired others to not only follow them but to contribute to a cause that changed the course of history. To be sure, his ideology transformed the lives of the inhabitants of our world.

Martin Luther King Jr. was assassinated in 1968 while in Memphis, Tennessee. He had traveled there to solidify support for striking workers, who viewed themselves as nonentities, placed into positions where they were being taken advantage of. It is noteworthy to mention that King died while working toward benefiting those he felt had been neglected.

It could be stated that Martin Luther King had tapped into God's anointing power and delivered a blow that transformed the face of humanity from within. His idea that "all people are equal in the eyes of God" unfolded the flower of freedom, equality, dignity, and respect for all life. Through his struggle against the laws of segregation, he convicted and changed unyielding hearts into thinking humans, for humanity, equality, and integrity had been reserved for the elite of his time.

We must ask ourselves if Martin Luther King's legacy would have remained if he had lived. It is a tantalizing question and one that warrants review. On the last night of his life, King gave a speech that proved eerily prophetic. In his book, *Martin Luther King Jr., Leader for Civil Rights*, Michael Schuman recalls King stating in part: "Like anybody, I would like to live a long life. Longevity has its place. But I'm not concerned about that now. I just want to do God's will ... I've seen the promised land. I may not get there with you" (p. 104). King had categorically stated that he wanted to do God's will. For him, it was a matter of serving his fellow man in order that his own life would improve for the better. Had he lived longer, we must venture to say that he would not have ceased his struggle. Perhaps his stature would have developed even further. It is conceivable that he accomplished his task to the fullest degree. Even so, his legacy has grown immensely over time.

In 1983 President Ronald Reagan signed a proclamation that made Martin Luther King's birthday a national and federal holiday. King's legacy is further enshrined as a cornerstone where future generations are humbled and protected by the bounds of human decency.

6

Legacy of the Caesars and the Roman Empire

Volumes of books, encyclopedias, manuscripts, and movies have expounded on the glory that was Rome. Perhaps more than any other empire, Rome and the emperors it produced affected the entire world as none other. Without a doubt, the legacy of ancient Rome and its caesars has influenced our modern day civilization through its methods of government, art, literature, and general way of life. It was the Roman Empire that created vast aqueducts that transported water from the Alps to its large cities—in effect, the world's first major plumbing system. It was Rome too that developed thoroughfare infrastructure that is still in use today.

The zenith of the Roman Empire saw its perimeters extended from Britannia in the north to Mesopotamia in the east, Egypt in the south, and present day Spain in the west. Rome was admired for its remarkable dimensions, as much then as it has been by the inhabitants of our era. The vastness of Rome encompassed cultures and nations of all kinds. It was to Rome's credit that the empire was aptly gifted at joining hedonistic tribes, as well as Babylonians, Greeks, and Egyptians, into the collective populace. It could be said that Rome enhanced the lives of those in the regions it occupied. Anyone within the boundaries of Rome could advance to a higher status. Even the higher echelons were available to those who fought hard enough for them. The names of Julius Caesar, Augustus, Nero, Hadrian, Trajan, and Constantine are the names of some who rose to such status.

Ancient Rome and its emperors had such an impact on history that it managed to interject itself into the Bible. Certainly, Caesar Augustus did not order it, but it is his name that is associated with the birth of Christ. We find history backing the Word of God, and the Word of God backing history. Such evidence is recorded in Luke 2:1 (KJV): "And it came to pass in those days, that there went out a decree from Caesar Augustus, that all the world should be taxed." Additionally, Paul wrote the book of Romans to the Romans themselves when the empire still existed. Even Jesus made a reference to Caesar, as we can see in Matthew 22:21 (KJV): "Render therefore unto Caesar the things which are Caesar's; and unto God the things that are God's." There are over eleven references to Caesar in the Word of God, which identify the times in which the authors lived in and the influence the empire produced.

It was an extraordinary characteristic that the Roman Empire was able to maintain the relative peace it needed within its borders. Its army was generally thought to maintain, at best, conscripts of only four hundred and fifty thousand.

This was the same army that covered and preserved an area of well over a million square miles for the empire. It was generally thought that this same army was sent to defend Rome from hostile foreigners and adversaries. This defensive posture caused the empire to grow from an insignificant, sixth-century, closed civilization to a colossal world empire in the first century. It is through this unique bearing that so many have sought to learn of its lasting legacy.

I believe that both the caesars of Rome and the empire itself have left a legacy and lasting influence on our present day civilization. Even our calendar bears reference to the names of Roman emperors: July for Julius Caesar, and August and October for Octavian Augustus.

Rome was founded, in legend, upon seven hills claimed by the twins Romulus and Remus. In a dispute over who should be king, Romulus killed Remus. He named the emerging new city after himself and called it Rome. The corresponding date of its founding is generally seen as 753 BC, although its accuracy cannot be authenticated. Scant evidence exists to support the account of Romulus and Remus. Both were probably created by contemporary historians of the time to explain their origins.

As the Roman Empire was both broad and extensive throughout history, I have provided an overview here. Legendary kings ruled the empire in its infancy from 753 BC to 509 BC, starting with its founder, Romulus, and extending to Superbus Tarquinius Priscus. Rome transformed from a monarchy to a republic in 509 BC, lasting as such for almost five hundred years. In 60 BC, the first triumvirate was formed with Gaius Julius Caesar, Pompey, and Crassus. Julius Caesar had absolute rule in Rome from 47 BC until he was murdered in 44 BC. It was not until the senate voted to give Octavius the title of Augustus, or "consecrated one," in 27 BC that Rome saw its first emperor. The republic came to an abrupt halt. The empire itself would last for over five hundred years, from 27 BC to AD 476.

It was during the reign of Gaius Octavius Augustus, commonly referred to as Caesar Augustus, when Jesus Christ was born. Augustus was also the first of the caesars to have his name mentioned in the Bible. Among Christians, his legacy has endured. In addition, Augustus was the first emperor of Imperial Rome, or the Roman Empire. He was referred to as Octavian, until he was granted the name Augustus in 27 BC. We will later focus on the legacy of Augustus, as he was considered the first, and perhaps the greatest, of the caesars.

Octavian was born in 63 BC as Gaius Octavius. He changed his name to Gaius Julius Caesar after Julius Caesar's death in 44 BC. His father, Gaius Octavius, was the first in his family to become a senator of Rome. His mother, Atia, was the niece of Julius Caesar. Atia was widowed in 59 BC, whereby the young Octavian was catapulted into a public career by Julius Caesar. Octavian accompanied Julius Caesar on many of his campaigns of war. Octavian traveled to Epirus in 44 BC to continue his military lessons and education. It was while in Epirus that Octavian first learned of Julius Caesar's murder.

Caesar's will had disclosed Octavian as his heir and adopted son. This posthumous declaration did not receive immediate official recognition. When vacancies occurred among the council's leading senatorial forces in the war of Mutina, Octavian was appointed by a reluctant senate to fill one of the positions. When this happened, his inheritance was recognized.

It is a common misconception that Julius Caesar was the first emperor of Rome. Julius Caesar was its first dictator; it was Octavian who became its first emperor. As we have mentioned earlier, Rome was a Republic until 27 BC. On the sixteenth of January in 27 BC, the senate voted to give Octavian the title of Augustus, or "anointed one." His elevation as the first Roman emperor signaled the end of the Roman republic.

Caesar Augustus left a legacy that was unparalleled in the history of the Roman Empire. In Michael Grant's tome, *The Roman Emperors*, we find attributes of the emperor: "Augustus was one of the most talented, energetic and skillful administrators that the world has ever known" (p. 15). Undeniably, Augustus's legacy left his subjects the benefit of advanced commerce and a much improved communications system. Although Christianity was unknown at the time, the Roman system would provide for the structure whereby Christianity would later flourish. It is a little-known fact that Augustus was also the author of several books. It is our misfortune that none have survived.

It is interesting to note that Augustus forbade the worship of himself as a god in Rome, but outside its perimeters, he encouraged the cult of the empire and Augustus. Perhaps he saw this as linking people to the benefits of the empire more than himself. It was common practice for citizens of Rome to worship and deify their emperors. He refused all such honors while he lived, yet he retained the title of "a son of a god" in reference to his adoption by Julius Caesar. It was to his credit that he retained his humanity in all of its forms.

Augustus was said to have left Rome full of marble—in the form of statues, monuments, buildings, and other construction. Many continued to fill the Forum even after he had dedicated it in 2 BC. The Temple of Mars Ultor became its grand masterpiece. It was an immense structure built by the emperor to show his revenge against Julius Caesar's death. It was but one such edifice designed to magnify the person of Augustus. Additionally, Augustus erected the Temple of Apollo, and the Theatre of Marcellus, vestiges of the glory of Rome. The Forum, originally intended to house the center of government, instead became a majestic overview of the achievements of Augustus. Even the name Augustus, a form of the word *august*, came to mean "majestic."

As the first emperor of Imperial Rome, Augustus remained a simple man. It is said that he had a simple army cot as his bed, one that he used for well over forty years. He also lived at his residence for that same length of time. Augustus ate simple foods that were usually reserved for the common people. He strove to avoid being ostentatious or having the appearance of being arrogant. To him, incongruous lavishness was to be avoided.

However, the foundation of the Roman emperor remains Augustus's proper legacy. His command and the good judgment built into his character caused the government to become powerful and stable. In his book, *The Caesars*, Allan Massie recalls Augustus's dying words: "How have I played my part in the comedy of life?" (p. 83). He must have played it well, for Augustus died in the month that bore his name: August 19, AD 14.

The legacy of the Roman Empire and its caesars would not be complete without considering its other emperors. While Augustus was inarguably one of its superior leaders, Nero was the antithesis of anything positive. Indeed, the despotic reign of Nero has burned the image of Christians being fed to the lions into people's minds. That has endured as his particular brand and legacy of cruelty and governance.

It is safe to say that Nero's reputation was regarded as so evil that he is widely known even today. Born in AD 37 as Lucius Domitius Ahenobarbus, he was later adopted by Emperor Claudius and took the family name of Nero. Initially, Nero was not in line to inherit the throne of Rome. His father, Gnaeus Ahenobarbus, was from one of the oldest leading families, and he had died when the young Lucius was only three. It was his mother, Agrippina, who would provide for his future ascendancy. Agrippina was the sister of Caligula and the future wife of Claudius, both emperors of Rome. During the reign of Claudius, Nero was formally adopted and named as the heir apparent.

Nero's ascendancy to the throne was further secured upon his marriage to Claudius's daughter, Octavia. Upon Claudius's death in AD 54, Nero became the emperor of Rome at the age of sixteen. Nero's reign began as a promising benefit to the empire. He guaranteed increased power and a greater role for the senate. He pledged, as a declaration, a return to the standards of Augustus. It was not to Nero's credit that he made such lofty promises, for those ideas and vision belonged to Seneca, who served as Nero's tutor and guide.

It could be said that Nero's legacy began with the death of Britannicus, Claudius's natural-born son. Although Nero had been declared emperor upon the death of Claudius, Britannicus remained an influential contender behind the throne. In a few short months after the death of Claudius, Nero had Britannicus poisoned while attending a banquet. Even though Nero blamed the death on a seizure, it was common knowledge that the emperor had disposed of his adversary. Additionally, he murdered two wives and his mother.

Nero's reputation as an executioner was solidified upon the death of his mother, Agrippina. The murder of his own mother can be seen as, perhaps, the single most infamous act of his time in power. Nero had a ship, designed especially for self-destruction, to carry Agrippina to her villas. On the first launch, the plan came into play, and the ship disintegrated. Agrippina merely swam to her home. Nero dispatched soldiers to complete his arrangement for her demise, and she was stabbed to death mercilessly. It is reported that she cried out, asking them to stab her in the womb from which Nero had been born.

The start of Nero's reign was marked by good judgment and control. Seneca, in addition to having served as Nero's tutor, guided the empire ably, along with Afranius Burrus, leader and commander of the Praetorian Guard. Upon the death of Burrus in AD 62, Seneca fell out of favor with Nero, eventually being forced to commit suicide in AD 65. Without his reliable and respected guides, Nero became the tyrannical ruler known throughout history. Trials were conducted for treasonous acts, and many people were condemned to banishment or suicide.

Nero is best remembered for an act he did not commit. The Great Fire, as it was known, engulfed most of Rome in AD 64. Started in the area of the Circus Maximus, it eventually consumed most of the city's districts, as well as the area in which the emperor lived. Nero had been in another region when the fire broke out, and he rushed back to organize assistance. It is a common misconception that Nero fiddled while Rome burned—as well as having started the fire. Although Nero was adept at playing his lyre, the story cannot be proven that he played it while Rome smoldered. Whether it is true or not, the story remains at the core of his legacy. This view has been reinforced by the fact that he built his Golden House on land that was cleared by the fire.

It was from this event that Nero launched his crusade against the fledgling Christian movement. The apostle Paul was executed by Nero in AD 64 and possibly served as a reminder that Christians were the culprits for maladies of all kinds. Persecutions began as games at the great Coliseum, wherein those who were considered followers of Christ were mauled and fed to the lions. Many were covered with animal skins and ripped apart by wild dogs. Moreover, they were used as human torches to serve as lamps at night. Nero blamed the fire on those who were called Christians, as he needed a scapegoat to deflect any personal blame. Many Christians went underground, hiding in caves and marking them with a fish symbol in order to find one another. As horrific as it was, it is conceivable that this very act of persecution served to ignite the passions of believers throughout the Roman Empire.

It is arguable that Nero's love of the arts and theater undermined the image of the emperor. It lent itself toward casting Nero as a nymph. Nero was known for performing poetry, songs, and his own compositions before large audiences while dressed in full theater costume. Those who had previously held the title of caesar had avoided such things. Their representations were preserved with a serious posture. This image of power displayed by Nero no doubt led to his being despised by the Roman legions.

Nero had a love for all things Greek. His Hellenistic tastes were reflected in his dress, style, and mannerisms. In his only foreign venture, Nero traveled to Greece to perform in theatrical productions. Prizes and awards were given to him in recognition. While he was in Greece, many senators, as well as those in union, instigated several plots against his life. One attempt in AD 65 and another in AD 66 resulted in the executions and banishment of conspirators among many ranks and levels of society. As a direct result of those colleagues, relations between Nero and the senate became nonexistent. It is interesting to note that while Nero's troubles were with the senate, he remained popular with the wide majority of citizens of Rome and the empire.

In June of AD 68, events culminated into Nero's being threatened with arrest by his own soldiers. While in hiding, he committed suicide by stabbing himself in the neck. After such a promising start, Nero created his own legacy by virtue of overindulgence and insecurity.

Thus far, we have seen some examples and types of emperors that the Roman Empire produced. Each left his own legacy, highlighting what men were capable of doing—for good or bad. Additional caesars included Tiberius, Hadrian, Diocletian, and—perhaps the one who had the greatest influence on Christianity—Constantine. It could be stated that the reign of Constantine marked a definite turning point in the history of the Roman Empire. His enduring legacy remains and is founded in two events: he made Christianity the official religion of the Roman Empire, and he moved the capital from Rome to Constantinople, which is now present day Istanbul, Turkey.

The legacy of the caesar and the Roman Empire were intertwined, especially in the case of Constantine. It was Constantine who caused the transformation of the old Roman Empire into the new when the capital was transferred to Constantinople. Prior to his ascendancy as Caesar, Constantine saw the end of the persecution of Christians, and their proliferation throughout the empire.

Born in AD 272 or 273 (other sources place the date at AD 285) in the city of Naissus, Constantine, or Flavius Valerius Constantinus, was the son of the Caesar Constantius I and his wife Helena. Constantine first came into prominence at the court of the emperor Diocletian. His reputation as a first-rate officer was established when he served under his father's colleague and coruler, Galerius. When Constantius died, he was persuaded by his father's soldiers to accept his rightful place as ruler.

Upon Galerius's death in AD 311, Constantine defeated his various rivals to become the senior caesar, assuming the title of Augustus. Licinius, who ruled the eastern part of the empire, supported his cause and married Constantine's sister, Constantia, to solidify his own position. Constantine controlled the western portions of the empire, as Licinius oversaw the eastern part. Constantine ruled as joint emperor from AD 307 to 323 and as sole emperor from 323 until his death in 337.

Lavish in his bestowing of titles and privileged rank, Constantine was instrumental in reorganizing the Roman armies. Additionally, he continued Diocletian's tax and financial reforms throughout the empire. It remained a constant thought to both his predecessors and himself that Rome had ceased to be a feasible location for the capitol. Constantine was continuously on the move, and he had rendered Rome irrelevant to his long-term plans.

In AD 324 Constantine moved the capitol of the Roman Empire from Rome to the ancient Greek city of Byzantium. Upon the strategic Bosphorus straights between Europe and Asia, he founded and named the new city Constantinople. To the modern mind, it would appear that this particular move made no sense. However, in Constantine's day it provided proximity to heavily populated areas that enhanced trade and fostered further development. It was a move that shook the known world at the time. As part of his legacy, Constantine also planted the roots for the Byzantine Empire.

Although the moving of the center of power from Rome to Constantinople proved historic, it was Constantine's issuance of recognition for Christianity that remains his lasting legacy. His acknowledgment was founded in a vision he'd had before an impending battle. Constantine was converted to Christianity when he saw the cross superimposed over the sun. Its immediate effect caused him to order his soldiers to place the symbol of Christ upon their shields. While there is no reason to doubt Constantine's conversion, it must be noted that the foundation had been prepared in previous years.

When Diocletian and Galerius had launched one of the greatest persecutions ever seen against Christians (with the possible exception of Nero), the impact had left an indelible mark upon the mind of Constantine. We must also interject that Galerius was eaten alive by a deadly cancer, believing that it was a direct result of his policies of such discrimination. He rescinded his edicts and decrees upon his deathbed. It was also during his terminal illness that Galerius, along with Licinius and Constantine, issued the Edict of Serdica, which granted freedom of worship to all Christians.

The Edict of Milan was issued in AD 312 to further reiterate lenience for Christianity. Prior to its implementation, Constantine had been a follower of the sun god, which had been revered and worshipped by his ancestors. By the time the Edict of Milan had been enacted, Constantine had left no doubt as to his adherence to Jesus Christ as his personal Lord and Savior, and as the Son of God who had come in the flesh.

In AD 313, both Constantine and Licinius granted the return of church property to Christians in the eastern areas of the empire. Although it was considered a positive move forward, worship of old gods remained intact. Constantine's positives were also counterbalanced by his propensity to enforce his particular beliefs. One may find an example in the Donatist schism where Constantine enforced the decision of the attending council members by confiscation of Donatist churches and properties. Even though the statute was removed in 321, it demonstrated that Constantine was not exempt from persecuting Christians. It was not until 323, when Constantine would rule as sole emperor, that he truly began to promote his own brand of laws. Constantine would oversee the banning of gladiator contests, pagan sacrifices, and the eventual confiscation of idol relics. In addition, rigorous laws were ratified against prostitution and immorality. In AD 325, he attended the Council of Nicaea, in which a later council would be formed to introduce the Nicene Creed, a declaration stating that the Son, Jesus Christ, was of one substance with the Father.

Constantine saw himself as the guardian and protector of the Christian church. This belief was particularly manifested throughout the extensive architectural projects he embarked upon. He built the Church of the Holy Apostles in his new capitol, Constantinople. Its roof was designed in the form of the Christian cross, and it included burial places for Christian martyrs as well as a location for baptisms. He also built the original Basilica of Saint Peter in Rome, which was later destroyed to make room for the current structure.

Constantine's glittering legacy was otherwise marked by suspicions of treason. In AD 326 he ordered the executions of both his wife Fausta and Crispus, his oldest son from a previous marriage. Whether their executions stemmed as a result of treasonous acts or an alleged adulterous affair, it is said that Constantine suffered from endless guilt for having ordered the sentence to be carried out. This particular tragic event may have proved to be the catalyst that steered Constantine to Christianity. It is probable that Constantine may have felt that Christianity offered the forgiveness and peace he needed.

Another negative that was attached to Constantine's legacy was found in the tax system known as *chrysargyron*. A tax that was paid in gold and silver, Constantine had decreed that it was to be levied every four years. Failure to pay resulted in torture or beatings. The enactment of this levy would force fathers to prostitute their daughters for payment, or mothers to sell their children. Although Constantine was adept and able at conducting the financial affairs of the empire, it was to his discredit that the chrysargyron produced an effect opposite one of maintaining Christian values among his subjects.

Overall, Constantine's legacy has continued as a positive contribution toward Christianity. One may argue that his recognition of Christianity as a state-sponsored creed lessened the impact of conversion. Apathy was also an unintended consequence. However, his contribution as a Christian emperor instilled steadfast values into the early years of the church. Constantine was baptized by the Bishop of Nicomedia just prior to his death in AD 337.

In retrospect, the legacies of Augustus and Constantine both served to benefit humanity. Constantine benefited the church as well as the Christian population of his empire.

Politics and public life were transformed for the better. Christianity was given a platform from which many would hear the gospel. It is plausible that Christianity became more widely known as Constantine gave it official recognition. It could be stated that it also laid the foundation for our present day beliefs and practices. Augustus also lent his knowledge and skills to the improvement of communication, flourishing commerce, and the grandeur that remains of ancient Rome. From each legacy, modern civilization has benefited.

As for Nero, nothing can be seen that remains as a benefit to our present age. As mentioned earlier, he did enact reforms beneficial to his own time at the beginning of his reign. One could say that whatever little he did has been completely overshadowed by that which he should not have done. Nero's legacy, therefore, must be seen in light of one who performed for a circus. His alleged singing and fiddling while Rome burned, his unending attempts at theatrical performance, his immoral proclivities, and his persecution of Christians all served to create a caricature that is not easily forgotten. It remains his legacy when we are reminded of these events.

Overall, the Roman Empire benefited the world as a whole. It gave us the ideal of what it was like to be glorious, to be a model of governance and to create enormous edifices, transportation, water aqueducts, and lessons to be learned.

7

The Legacy of the Disciple Thomas

It is notable that we did not include Scripture when reviewing the legacy established by the caesars of Rome and by the Roman Empire itself. The exclusion of Scripture was intentional and highlighted the fact that the caesars of Rome replaced any semblance of a god. Constantine was the exception, as he set laws into place to fulfill what he saw as the will of God.

It is important to interject that the order of our chapters and the subjects we have examined thus far was also intentional. By following this particular order, we have seen glaring differences already in the legacies of each. Now we will evaluate the disciple Thomas, and we will find that his legacy is unique and must be reexamined and considered in a different light.

Perspicacity is required when evaluating a personage of history or his legacy. Lack of discernment has resulted in a great misalignment of Thomas's character, impacting his heritage throughout history. We have already seen an example of this in our discussion of the last czar of Russia, Nicholas II.

Although his character demonstrated compassion, concern, and overriding mercy, he is still known as "Bloody Nicholas."

Like Nicholas II, the disciple Thomas has been much maligned in his character and is in need of vindication. To secure his legacy in a positive light, we must discover what we know of Thomas. We must also discuss the misalignment of his character and attempt his vindication through his calling. It is important to study Thomas's responses throughout Scripture. To do otherwise would be to leave his reputation as it has been perceived for over two thousand years—as "doubting Thomas."

Thomas is mentioned in a total of eight passages in the New Testament. Four of them contain lists of the apostles where his name is included. We first read about Thomas in Matthew 10:2–3 where it states, "These are the names of the twelve apostles: first Simon (who is called Peter) and his brother Andrew; James son of Zebedee, and his brother John; Philip and Bartholomew; Thomas and Matthew the tax collector" (NIVSB). As far as gospel history is concerned, we know nothing of Thomas—where he worked or where his residence was located. We do know, however, that Acts 1:11 (NIV) states, "'Men of Galilee,' they said, 'Why do you stand here looking into the sky?'" (NIV). We can ascertain from this passage that Thomas, in all probability, was Galilean and most certainly a Jew, as all of the disciples were gathered together prior to Jesus' ascension. In Herbert Lockyer's book, *All the Apostles of the Bible*, we find the following: "From legendary material we gather that Thomas was born of poor parents, brought up in the trade of fishing, gained a useful education, and was instructed in the knowledge of Scriptures; whereby he learned wisely to govern his life and manners ... Because his name is paired with that of Matthew, there are those who suggest that they may have been twin brothers" (p. 175).

Thomas was a Hebrew name, and its Greek equivalent, *Didymus*, was translated "a twin." It is therefore easy to see how Herbert Lockyer would come to the conclusion that Thomas was a twin, possibly related to Matthew. Further information on Thomas is found in Larry Richards' book, *Every Man in the Bible*, which says, "A relatively strong tradition tells us that Thomas traveled to India and established a church there that has continued into the twenty-first century" (p. 185). We can therefore surmise, from the scant information we do have, that Thomas continued on in ministry long after Jesus left. What little we do know, as discovered later, will prove sufficient in understanding Thomas. It is in the book of John where Thomas is saved from total obscurity, making him a reality, as we shall see further on.

Of all the apostles, it can be said that Thomas was perhaps the most maligned. Indeed, many only recognize him as "doubting" Thomas. When thinking of Thomas, people generally connect him with being a "doubter" or "reckless." This is an unfortunate legacy for Thomas and one that we must attempt to change. The nature of these characterizations may be found in the fact that a negative usually outweighs the positive. Nero's legacy is a case in point. Another example can be seen in John 11:16 where Jesus, having heard that Lazarus had died, was then confronted with Thomas's statement.

In Eugene H. Peterson's version of the Bible, *The Message*, Thomas's declaration sounds hopeless: "Then said Thomas, which is called Didymus, unto his fellow disciples, 'Let us go, that we may die with him.'"

On the surface, the negative aspects of Thomas's statement can be seen as too pessimistic. It seems that Thomas had given up all hope. His statement could also be misconstrued as meaning that there was no other way out. It could therefore be seen as a reckless statement in its entirety. When the two versions of Thomas's statement are compared, we see that one can have a greater negative connotation than the other.

Let us, however, view his statement in a different light. It could be argued that Thomas spoke up because he did not want to hinder Jesus in doing what He desired, though it might cost Thomas and the disciples their lives. In this perspective, his statement might be seen as a brave decision rather than a reckless statement. It is noteworthy to find that Thomas did not run for his life afterward.

The association of Thomas being a doubter is again found in the book of John. John 20:24–25 (NIVSB) says, "Now Thomas (called Didymus), one of the Twelve, was not with the disciples when Jesus came. So the other disciples told him, 'We have seen the Lord!' But he said to them, 'Unless I see the nail marks in his hands and put my finger where the nails were, and put my hand into his side, I will not believe it.'" Here we might infer that Thomas's absence showed his lack of will to follow Jesus, that he might have feared the consequences of following Jesus after His death. Subsequently, his response— after having not been with Jesus and the disciples—can easily be seen as one rife with doubts. We must ask ourselves, would we have responded as Thomas did?

Again, seen in a different light, one can see Thomas's reaction as one that would simply demand facts about the Lord he had been serving and following. We find that Thomas was later compelled to be with the disciples, thus exonerating him of any faults or shortcomings he may have experienced previously.

In John 14:5 (NIVSB), we once again find Thomas: "Thomas said to him, 'Lord, we don't know where you are going, so how can we know the way?'" This was at the occasion of the last Passover meal that Jesus shared with His disciples. Thomas undoubtedly felt sadness, and like the rest of the disciples, he did not want Jesus to leave. Thomas's question reveals his quest in the continuing search for knowledge, in that he asked the Lord where He was going and how they too could know the way. Critics of Thomas may be quick to point out that Thomas had not been listening to the Lord. Had not the Lord Himself spent time teaching them? Thomas could be viewed here as missing information, for Jesus stated the answers needed: "In my Father's house are many mansions" (John 14:2). Thomas may have been overly cautious in accepting the truth and even slow in his thinking. However, it must be established that here was a disciple, chosen by Jesus, who was moving steadily onward and who later showed faith and zeal that would be needed again and again. Indeed, it was to Thomas's credit that he never surrendered. He never allowed himself to capitulate to the circumstances or situation at hand. It is evident that the true character and nature of Thomas emerged early.

In Walter A. Henrichsen's book, *Disciples Are Made Not Born*, he attests to the following: "Making disciples takes time. It cannot be done through a series of lectures, or training seminars, nor by reading a book. It cannot be rushed. Each must be molded and fashioned individually by the Spirit of God" (p. 107). Henrichsen had to have thought of Thomas when he wrote such a statement. It can explain why so many have rushed to judgment on Thomas; they have failed to see what God was doing in Thomas's life and how he responded. It is a further testament to Thomas's character that the Lord too saw in him a candidate and character worthy to call His disciple and apostle. We must stipulate that the Lord's endorsement is higher than any other.

In Gene A. Getz's book, *The Apostles Becoming Unified through Diversity*, Getz makes the following assessment: "People with pessimistic attitudes are also normally direct and blunt and very cerebral, finding it hard to make the jump from human reasoning to faith." Initially, Thomas may have been unable to take the steps of faith needed; his human reasoning barred him. Additionally, his character flaws of doubt, fear, and reckless statements may have prevented him from being the apostle and disciple that he could be. However, we must reevaluate this negative conception, for it has been the one that has unjustly determined the legacy of Thomas.

A legacy need not stay in intact, particularly if it is a harmful one. We must emphasize that Thomas truly did possess all that was needed to live up to his calling. We must also mention again that it was the Lord who had identified him.

Thomas was selected as one of only twelve to become a disciple and apostle. In William Barclay's book, *Jesus as They Saw Him*, the true definition of an apostle is discovered: "The Greek word for apostle is apostolos, from the verb apostellein, meaning 'sent forth,' or 'despatched'" (p. 321). Jesus truly "sent out" the original twelve apostles, "dispatched" as representatives of Himself. Thomas, having been chosen by Jesus himself, surely had the Master's confidence, insight, and trust from the beginning. In spite of what Thomas would say or do, he had Jesus' seal of approval from the onset of his calling.

In the book of John, Thomas is further vindicated. In John 20:28 (NIVSB), we see a dramatic illustration of Thomas's true character: "Thomas said to him, 'My Lord and my God!'" Thomas's statement after seeing Jesus validates him not as a doubter but rather a believer who was passionately ready to follow Jesus, even to his death. At his first sight of Jesus, any skepticism experienced by Thomas evaporated into unabashed devotion. Thomas, although only briefly shown in the New Testament, shines through as a person worth emulating. First and foremost, his loyalty showed, for he was ready to die for Jesus. Jesus had become so significant to Thomas that he was willing to follow the Master at all costs. Second, although Thomas possessed an amount of uncertainty when questioning Jesus, he exemplified an inquiring spirit. He questioned matters of faith, yearning to know more, while drawing closer to the Lord.

A further vindication of Thomas is illustrated in Grant R. Jeffrey's book, *Jesus: The Great Debate*: "The apostle Thomas was stabbed with a spear in India during one of his missionary trips to establish the church in the subcontinent" (p. 175). It would hardly befit Thomas to continue to be called a "doubter," having so gloriously faced a martyr's death.

Carolyn Nystrom's tome, *New Testament Characters*, raises a question: "How might a period of doubt, such as Thomas experienced, have a long term positive effect?" The answer may lie in what we have found in the life of Thomas. Initially riddled with questions, doubts, and fears, Thomas transformed into the apostle that Jesus had first recognized. We must interject, that it is God who knows the hearts of men. He is also the one who can see what lies ahead. Furthermore, the Spirit of God knows all, sees all, and searches all things. The selection of Thomas—first as a disciple and then as an apostle—serves as a true indicator of God's expressive love for humanity. With Thomas, as well as ourselves, God looks beyond our faults and takes full view of the end result.

Thomas was able to show the fearlessness of his devotion, and he rose to meet the calling that Jesus had placed upon him. Thomas also proved that he was able to stand, in spite of every conceivable obstacle placed in his path. We must therefore conclude that what Thomas lacked in character, he made up in indomitable courage and a need to establish the facts. The establishment of facts has served as the foundation for ascertaining the truth.

Thomas did not reject the actuality that the disciples had seen Jesus; he merely wanted to confirm that fact by seeing the Lord himself. Thomas became the conqueror, the victor, and the "swordsman of faith." Much to his credit, Thomas stood firm, resulting in the proliferation of the gospel of Jesus Christ around the world.

Perhaps the legacy of Thomas should be revised. Certainly, there was much more to what he accomplished than what is written in the Word of God. We know through historical and traditional sources that Thomas served under King Gondophares, a monarch who was known as the "King of the Indians." We have mentioned that it was in India where Thomas met his death as a martyr. What we did not mention was the fact that Thomas was kneeling in prayer when the spear plunged into his body. If his legacy is based on anything, it should rely upon the fact that he met his death stoically.

It is said that Thomas was the disciple who was responsible for the conversion of the "three Kings of the East," the same monarchs who brought gifts to the infant Jesus. Thomas was buried with another king that he had converted: King Sagamon. It was another testament to his legacy that has been lost or obscured by the "doubt factor." Memorials, statues, and churches have been erected in Thomas's memory throughout the world. A church—housing a relic purported to be a fragment of his bones—was erected and is still seen today in India.

What should the legacy of Thomas depict? We have made a compelling case. Standing for the cause of Christ should be enough to leave a lasting legacy that benefits all humanity.

8

Adolf Hitler and His Legacy of Destruction

Perhaps no other name has conjured up more heated feelings of loathing, fear, and disgust—or even admiration by his followers—than that of Adolf Hitler. The demonic nature of his gifts enabled a crowd to worship him in delirious frenzy. It facilitated his path in attempting to conquer the world. His legacy was one of destruction, terror, and mayhem. Hitler rose to the highest position in the German hierarchy, and he ruled supreme over more territory than that of the French emperor Napoleon, Charlemagne, or even Alexander the Great. It proved to serve as his demise, but he nevertheless left the world an impression of his evil.

It is difficult to imagine how one individual could have inflicted such evil upon the psyche of humanity. Hitler erupted upon the scene like an earthquake, suddenly and without warning. His was a life initially content with obscurity. He had lived in small hovels in Austria, scarcely existing as he sold postcards to survive. It can be argued that his life directly resulted in the deaths of over fifty million souls. He destroyed anyone who obstructed his vision of the world, and he took all means necessary to enforce his will as a dictator.

To this point, we have reviewed legacies that were both beneficial and detrimental to humanity. Hitler's was a legacy that wreaked havoc and left no enhancement whatsoever. We must ask ourselves what would impel a person to engage in the annihilation of humanity—and the Jews in particular? Were Hitler's crimes a result of historical forces or ideology?

We are reminded of Esther's defense against the wicked Haman, who also sought to destroy the Jews. Hitler's policies proved far more caustic. We can surmise that Hitler murdered the Jewish people not because he was obligated but because he wanted to. His systematic annihilation of the Jewish population within his realm resulted in the deaths of over six million people. He established the infamous concentration camps throughout Europe. They have stood as proof of the holocaust he unleashed. It is his legacy that millions were sent to the showers of Auschwitz and Treblinka to be gassed to death with cyanide.

If there is one shining spot in the morass of Hitler's devastation, it would be the resulting rebirth of the State of Israel. The ancient land became a homeland once again for the remnant of Jews who survived World War II. Although Hitler did not survive to see it birthed into existence, one is tempted to contemplate his reaction if he had. He would have seen it as the opposite effect of his intentions, that being the destruction of those he hated: God's appointed people.

Nothing can explain, on the human level, the destructive path that Hitler left: psychological disparity, human dysfunction and genealogy, and ideology bent on supremacy over all. Spiritually, Hitler's condition is easily identifiable as demonic possession. In Matthew 17:15 (NIV), we are reminded of the man who came to Jesus, asking for mercy: "Lord have mercy on my son: for he is lunatic, and sore vexed." His son was insane as a result of demon possession. Was Hitler insane through possession?

As we have mentioned before, Nero took delight in using Christians as human torches to light up the night sky in the Coliseum. Likewise, Hitler was decidedly delirious, in that those who opposed his plans were later found exterminated. He undoubtedly ordered the execution of Dietrich Bonhoeffer, a famously outspoken theologian of Hitler's time. Bonhoeffer refused to parrot from his pulpit the Nazi ideology that glorified the fuehrer of Germany and espoused nationalist socialism. It cost him his life in 1945 when he was sent to a concentration camp. Bonhoeffer was a martyr who had kept his eyes upon the eternal things of God.

It is worth mentioning that Dr. Richard Land quotes Dr. Martin Luther King Jr. in his article, "For Faith and Family," connecting Hitler and Dietrich Bonhoeffer: "If your opponent has a conscious, then follow Gandhi and nonviolence. But if your enemy has no conscious like Hitler, then follow Bonhoeffer" (p. 1). During the rule of Nazism, Hitler ordered all churches to place the swastika and the Nazi flag upon their altars. Those not found in compliance were subjected to heavy fines or closure. Oftentimes, pastors and church officials disappeared without a trace.

It is necessary to lay the groundwork of Hitler's life in order to seek an explanation for his legacy of destruction. We know that Hitler was evil, but *why* was he evil? What would be the foundation and predilection of such a wicked course? Perhaps there can be no definitive answers to such questions, but we can recognize at least a stark reality between what is good and what is evil.

In Ron Rosebaum's book, *Explaining Hitler,* he quotes Hitler. "People must not know who I am," he was reported to have ranted when he learned of one of the early investigations into his family history. "They must not know where I come from" (p. 4). Indeed, Hitler was successful at obscuring his past during his day, and many people were oblivious of his country of origin. Such obscurity served to expand the many rumors and slander that followed Hitler's rise to fame. Conversely, it provided the mystical and legendary status he had long sought after.

The secrecy that surrounded Adolf Hitler began with the name change of his father, Alois Schicklgruber. It is unclear who Hitler's grandfather was, and it is alleged that Alois changed his name to Hitler in order to procure proceeds from a purported will. Rumors persisted that Alois was subsidized by a Jewish family during his youth, garnering speculation that Adolf Hitler had Jewish roots. Hitler denied this as absurdity in 1930 during an internal investigation. Such disregard also lends credibility. While he was dictator of Germany in 1936, Hitler had the town of Dollersheim, Austria, obliterated. The inhabitants were effectively evacuated, and the settlement was rendered faceless. The infinitesimal Austrian hamlet had the unique distinction of being the origin of Hitler's ancestors. It was also deemed to be the only source that could have substantiated such claims. Why had Hitler given the order for such destruction? Was it his attempt to eliminate any connections to his possible Jewish roots? Other versions of the account testify that the Russians destroyed Dollersheim in 1945.

Hitler's father married his mistress and niece, Klara Polzl, in the winter of 1885. Klara bore Alois four sons and two daughters, of which only one daughter and one son survived. Although Adolf had one stepbrother and one stepsister, it remains an enigma that the surviving son was Adolf Hitler. In those days, it was not an uncommon thing for so many children to die in infancy. Adolf was born in Branau am Inn, Austria, on April 20, 1889.

Adolf Hitler developed a strong penchant for all things German when his family moved to the old German city of Passau in Austria. He learned the accents of established Germans who had settled there long ago. This would explain Hitler's appeal to native Germans when he campaigned for office in Germany years later. The fact that he was from Austria was obscured completely when he spoke before masses of adoring Germans.

Early in life, Adolf developed a penchant for arguing with his fellow schoolmates. It would foster a seed within him to seize the lead position when he later joined the Nationalist Socialist Movement. He was also fascinated with the Benedictine monastery to which his school was attached. It is a little known fact that Hitler actually had a high regard for the traditions of the church and had contemplated joining the monastical order. It is said that he actually admired the worship services it produced. The same Benedictine monastery displayed a coat of arms over the archway of the gate. Belonging to the abbot of the school, the center of it contained a swastika. It is probable that it produced in Hitler's mind the original the Nazi symbol that would spread fear across the world.

A pattern developed in Hitler's character as a young boy when his older brother Edmund died in 1900. Hitler turned inward and allowed himself to meditate upon the cemetery wall near Edmund's grave. During the same year, Hitler attended a higher category of school that drew him further from his family. It was also during this period that he formed his artistic talents. It became a necessary diversion during the many days of pain and seclusion that he would experience. Until the end of his life, Hitler would continue to declare conflict upon the world he reviled.

As a young boy, Hitler read books that depicted the slaughter of Indians by white Americans. One of his favorite characters, created by author Karl May, was a legendary Wild West hero who quoted the Bible to rationalize his massacre of inferior races. May's male protagonist indiscriminately slaughtered any of the warring tribes he judged to be inferior. We can see a clear pattern of influence upon Hitler's later decisions in life. Scripture taken out of context proved dangerous indeed. Was it possible that the adventures created by Karl May later directed Hitler's insane and inexcusable vengeance toward the carnage of humanity? Proverbs 22:6 (KJV) states, "Train up a child in the way he should go: and when he is old, he will not depart from it." Could Hitler's parents have neglected to guide his inclinations, thereby causing the destructive seed within him to germinate over the years? Perhaps, in his own mind, Hitler was deliberately meting out his own form of destruction by acting as the vaunted character created by Karl May.

In the winter of 1903, Hitler's father died and left him as the male head of the family. It is a misconception that the family was in dire straights. Hitler's father had provided for them by virtue of his pension as an Austrian customs official. Hitler comforted himself by delving more into his school studies and by exploring the virtues of religion. We have gained some insight into his beliefs, a system of absolutes that were kept intact until his death. In Robert Payne's book, *The Life and Death of Adolf Hitler*, we can see the result of such fixed convictions: "He had read somewhere that Saint Anthony flagellated himself in order to master the desires of the flesh, and this seemed to him the height of Christian absurdity" (p. 35). At an early age, Hitler formulated his opinion that Christianity was to be attended to by clerics and elderly women.

Hitler's mother died in December of 1907, which provided him the opportunity to move to Vienna. It is said that upon her death, Hitler lost any affection he may have had for humanity. Along with the backdrop of Vienna, this loss proved critical in the formation of his opinions. Vienna was rife with protestations and charges against Jews as being subversive activists. The general population viewed Jews as having control over all banking systems and exerting undue influence over the press. Hitler was indubitably influenced by such public sentiment. It was also in Vienna that he attempted to pursue his floundering career as an artist. He was rejected by several art academies more than once. It would later solidify his hatred and hostility against any form of authority. The characteristics of the future Hitler were already recognizable.

In the midst of Vienna's mayhem, Hitler searched for an ideology through which he could vent his antipathy toward society. During his earlier school years, he had been exposed to anti-Semitic attitudes. Students had adopted the German nation by greeting one another with the Germanic "Heil." His history teacher had familiarized him with his own hatred of amalgamated races and nations. Hitler carried forward these ideas to the pinnacle of the German nation.

In the year 1913, Hitler moved from Vienna to Munich. Munich also flourished with anti-Semitism and further inflamed his passions against the Jews. It was also in the atmosphere of Munich that Kaiser Wilhelm II called for the mobilization of all able-bodied men. In 1914, with war upon the horizon, Hitler responded by enlisting in the Imperial Army of Germany.

Hitler supplied messages as a courier between the German troops. He earned the Iron Cross when he captured a squad of French soldiers by surprise. He was to use this later as a legitimate claim toward his involvement in German politics. His future followers gave him their loyalty as a result. Hitler was to declare later that the war had transformed him. It had reinforced within him the idea that his was a special mission.

World War I had made its own contribution in formulating Hitler's ideas. Hitler had declared that the enemy had won through its propaganda machine. Indeed, the German public was certain of their adversary's superiority in the field of public opinion. There can be no doubt that that same apparatus, employed during the Third Reich, was a direct result of the World War I. That same superiority factor was embedded in Hitler's mind.

The defeat of Germany in 1918 resulted in the establishment of the Weimar Republic. Hitler's anti-Semitic views were heightened, as most Germans blamed the Jews for their defeat at the hands of the Allies. In 1919 Hitler became an ardent supporter of disenchanted soldiers, and he blamed both the new German government and the Jews for their plight. His argument cited the cause of their bitterness and disgust: the betrayal of Germany by internal forces, the threat of Jewish dominion, the rise of Marxist-Leninism, and the humiliation brought about by the Treaty of Versailles. Each became an unbearable link in a chain that served only to inflame the discontent that had risen to the surface.

Hitler found a greater voice through his involvement with the German Workers' Party. This party was made up of middle-class, skilled workers, railroad employees, students, and discharged soldiers. Women attended meetings, particularly after Hitler became its main speaker. The party had been formed with a vision to unite the classes of German society. It favored the socialization of large trust funds and the abolition of certain banking practices. The enticement of improved working conditions lured many toward its cause. Hitler not only became its lead spokesman but its most ardent supporter. The premise of serving the common good would later become the policy of the National Socialist Party. The German Workers' Party was radically anti-Semitic and did not recognize Jews as German citizens. The leaders of the German Workers' Party recognized Hitler's oratory skills. Hitler saw the German Workers' Party as an opportunity to advance both his agenda and economic status.

Hitler became the chairman of the propaganda committee, which was designed to further the goals and views of the German Workers' Party. Hitler recognized his ability to transform his listeners into followers and disciples. He realized that the spoken word was made more effective through the written word. The foundations were laid early for the crucial advancement of his thoughts and policies. He would later use lighting and stage effects for dramatization; it highlighted his agenda for the greatest effect. Other military leaders sought Hitler's help, recognizing his leadership over the masses. They understood that the masses were needed to realize their goals. Hitler formed alliances that worked to his advantage.

Before 1922 the German Workers' Party changed its name to the National Socialist Deustch Arbeiterpartei (NSDAP), or the National Socialist German Party. By 1923 the party had grown to well over fifty thousand members. Hitler was elected its chairman in June of 1921. Hitler had himself elected as the sole authority, and he remained as such until the NSDAP morphed into the Nazi movement. Part of the strength of the NSDAP resulted from its merging with other parties. The NSDAP stipulated that Adolf Hitler continue as its supreme authority. It remained anti-Semitic, with the overriding goal of enforcing its political agenda throughout Germany.

The Weimer Republic was critically unstable in January of 1923. Severe unemployment, massive strikes, and political upheaval placed the NSDAP into a more favorable and prominent position nationwide. The occupation of the Ruhr by the French army gave them a sympathetic following.

In November of 1923, Hitler led his followers into a revolt against the German government. His attempted uprising caused Hitler to be arrested and the NSDAP to be outlawed. Hitler wrote his infamous book, *Mein Kampf,* or "My Struggle," while in prison. *Mein Kampf* was Hitler's testimony of his personal life, as well as his political views and vision of a utopian society. It was used to oppose any other writings that had stereotyped Hitler. A subsequent trial sentenced Hitler to five years in Landsberg prison. He was released in December of 1924. Following his release, Hitler revived the NSDAP.

The years that followed inspired Hitler to clarify his vision and purpose for the NSDAP. The stock market crash in the United States had caused a worldwide depression. Germany was critically impacted throughout its economy and was unable to export its products. Bankruptcies and lack of investor confidence, coupled with an agricultural crisis, introduced a fertile foundation for the policies that Hitler advocated. Hitler viewed these catastrophic events as an opportunity to further advance his political career.

In 1930 the National Socialist Party gained eighteen percent of the seats in the German parliament. Two years later, in 1932, the party became the strongest contingency in the German governing body, gaining 230 seats, or 37 percent of the Reichstag. Hitler was poised to become the chancellor of Germany. He had used his propaganda skills to reveal to the German people that he was the leader and savior of their cause to restore Germany. The people were on the brink of following his direction wherever he would guide them.

January of 1933 saw the world take its historic turning point, as Hitler was elected chancellor of Germany. It marked the end of the Weimar Republic and ushered in the Nazi Party, also known as the NSDAP. Hitler received 92 percent of the votes, which caused him to perceive his agenda as a mandate from the German people. The stage was set for Hitler's unchallenged rule as a dictator.

Hitler's seizure of power was initiated with the burning of the Reichstag building. He blamed this event on the German Communist Party and those who had opposed him. Hitler convinced the German president, Paul von Hindenburg, to enact drastic restrictions and reduction of civil rights. Subsequently, the powers of cabinet ministers were limited, as were those of parliamentary members. After the rebuilding of the new Reichstag, Hitler consolidated his authority and passed a law through the legislature called the Enabling Act. This law eliminated most parliamentary functions and gave Hitler more control to legislate. Hitler and his cabinet gained unrestricted rule to conduct foreign policy.

The result of this disastrous policy eliminated all German parties except the Nazi Party. The Social Democrats were the only contingent to vote against the enactment. By 1933 the National Socialist German Workers' Party was the only party left in Germany. It became Hitler's voice and arm for the endorsement of his goals and views. The Reichstag became ineffective. Hitler worked to incorporate former members of parties that were now defunct. He confiscated the assets of German unions and enforced the transfer of powers from the state to the central government.

The seeds of destruction were sown early in Hitler's life. We have seen clearly the establishment of disparaging events and thoughts that guided Hitler's every endeavor. It is interesting to note that his early reliance on the teachings of his abbot—a role model intended for the good—instead turned Hitler toward destruction. Although it was not the only factor, it was perhaps the most destructive one. The teachings of Hitler's abbot fostered the anti-Semitism that dictated his every deed and action.

Could Hitler have avoided his pathway to destruction? Was he molded irrevocably by the events and circumstances of his day? His rise to power seemed meteoric and only served to solidify his early formulated thoughts. Anti-Semitism had already taken root well before Hitler gained absolute power. We are reminded of the axiom that absolute power corrupts absolutely. Was Hitler already corrupted?

Our answer may be found in the fact that Hitler wasted no time in amassing his political strength. Every threat that beleaguered him was quickly resolved through creative means—or by sheer will. Proverbs 11:11 (KJV) states, "By the blessing of the upright the city is exalted; but it is overthrown by the mouth of the wicked." It has been said that Hitler spoke so effectively that he mesmerized millions with his words. We must ask again: was Hitler demon possessed? He certainly was considered wicked. We must consider his reaction to his ascendancy to power and his relationship with some of the churches of Germany that sanctioned his policies. Many in the church turned a blind eye in the interest of self-preservation.

It is plausible that Hitler, like all tyrants, dictators, or despots, saw himself as the new messiah of Germany. This, of course, presented itself as a thorny issue when he was dealing with the religious establishments. For example, the Catholic Church already had formidable power throughout Germany. Hitler was able to surmount any challenges that the Catholic Church posed by issuing what was called the Concordat. The Concordat was an agreement between the Catholic Church and Hitler's government whereby the German state was exclusive in the issuance of its political policies, and the Catholic Church was sovereign over its own affairs. It was set up, ostensibly, as a protection against the Communist threat in Germany. Pope Pius XII was gripped with the menace of Communism and was unwilling to combat any threat from the Nazi government.

The Protestant religions were more of an annoyance to Hitler, who appointed weak and submissive leaders to obey his will. Most were ineffective in gaining an outspoken voice against him, although there were a few exceptions. Clerical opposition, which included resistance within the Catholic and Protestant churches, was not completely muted or subservient. With the possible exception of the Vatican, ministers and priests alike opposed the supremacy of both Hitler and the National Socialist Party. We have mentioned Dietrich Bonhoeffer, who remained defiant until the end of his life. Pastor Martin Niemoller was another such individual. Niemoller was sentenced to a concentration camp for his audacity in directly confronting Hitler. Martin Niemoller remained incarcerated in a concentration camp until the very end of World War II.

Hitler's legacy of destruction began in earnest in 1933. In that year, labor unions were dissolved and books were burned. Additionally, a law was passed that made it a crime to form new political parties. Germany further isolated itself when it withdrew from the League of Nations. Hitler remained unopposed.

The Sturmabteilung, a military organization better known as the SA, was designed and organized for Hitler's political purposes. The SA was unconventional in combating internal problems. Captain Ernst Rohm served as its highest person in command. The organization's methods included assassination, political intimidation, and physical violence. Originally formed to advance Hitler's goals, the SA evolved as its own separate entity. Its new vision was to gain more political control. As its influence increased, Hitler was faced with a military coalition that threatened his power. Indeed, it was larger than the German army itself. Hitler's legacy of destruction was further consolidated when he ordered the murders of Rohm and his top leadership. By 1934 Hitler ruled with little or no resistance.

The German president, Paul von Hindenburg, died in August of 1934. Hitler seized the moment and became both chancellor and fuehrer, or "Supreme German Leader." The armed forces of Germany swore allegiance to him on the day that followed. Hindenburg's death had provided a doorway for Hitler's road to absolute supremacy. Hitler also masked his penchant for such power in the guise of several promises. He was astute enough to realize that there were voices that needed to be pacified. Hitler had appealed to the Christian population of Germany, encouraging them to take the lead on moral issues. Many were promised peace.

From the onset, Hitler's goal was the complete domination of Europe and the requisition of lands that Germany had lost under the Treaty of Versailles. Hitler employed millions of Germans through his secret rearmament of the nation. Here, we must interject the words of 1 Thessalonians 5:3 (KJV): "For when they shall say, Peace and safety; then sudden destruction cometh upon them, as travail upon a woman with child; and they shall not escape." Surely the people of Germany were pacified through deception. What else could explain Hitler's unabated control and manipulation? The seeds of devastation and the plunging of the world into a second global war were accomplished by such tactics—even though peace and safety had been promised.

The nations of the world had been horrified by the damage of World War I. Humanity was not prepared for such an onslaught once again. Conceivably, this explained the blind eye that so many turned toward Hitler as he marched forward uninterrupted toward world conquest. He saw himself as

Frederick the Great—and the messiah of Germany. Many thought him to be the Antichrist. Most of Germany, however, followed him without question.

Increasing employment might also explain why Hitler was unchallenged. It was one of Hitler's most astonishing achievements. While the rest of the world was mired in an economic depression, Germany's overheated economy was a miracle in the making. Although it presented problems of another kind, the populace accepted his every word and placed their trust in him. Hitler's remedy was to annex the Sudetenland, Austria, and parts of Czechoslovakia.

By 1939 almost 50 percent of the gross national product was dedicated to German rearmament. By this time, Hitler had regained the entire territory it had lost through World War I and the Treaty of Versailles. With Germany prepared for any outcome, Hitler had pressed his demand for the annexation of the Sudetenland and parts of Czechoslovakia. The imminent threat compelled Britain's prime minister, Neville Chamberlain, to meet with Hitler. An unsuccessful outcome resulted in Chamberlain's employing the French premier, Daladier, for further negotiations.

Held in Munich, Hitler expanded the conference to include Benito Mussolini, Italy's Fascist dictator. A great admirer of Mussolini, Hitler had attached enormous importance to his attendance. Indeed, Mussolini played an important part in creating what later became known as the Munich Agreement. The Sudetenland was subsequent to the eventual annexation of Czechoslovakia. Hitler had no opposition when his troops entered the capital of Prague. Chamberlain had left for Britain, convinced that he had obtained peace for the world.

The Soviet-German Nonaggression Treaty of 1939 was designed as a ruse for the eventual German invasion of the Soviet Union. Joseph Stalin, the Soviet Union's tyrannical dictator for life, was inclined to receive whatever trade and credits that Nazi Germany would extend. Stalin's objectives were designed to upgrade his flailing economy. Hitler had other aims; he would only honor an agreement if it suited his purposes. His ultimate goal was to achieve additional land through the invasion of Russia itself.

Neville Chamberlain had warned in a speech before the British parliament that Britain and France would declare war on Germany for any further territorial designs or invasions. Hitler had dismissed the probability that both would come to the aid of his next victim, Poland. On September 1, 1939, Hitler invaded the hapless nation of Poland. Many have speculated as to what might have been done to avert war, but we must conclude that Hitler's agenda was formulated when he took power in Germany. The goal, all along, had been to regain what Germany had lost, not only its territorial claims but its pride and honor as a nation. Hitler wanted no less than a restored Germany—and much more than what he was claiming.

We have mentioned that Hitler's legacy of destruction started long before war was declared. It continued until the end of World War II. In Germany, German Jews were singled out for persecution. The closing of Jewish businesses became commonplace. Jews who opposed Hitler were sent to reorientation camps and, eventually, concentration camps. Homes and properties were confiscated, while those identified as Jews were forced to wear the Star of David on their clothing. *Kristallnacht*, or "Crystal Night," became famous in November of 1938. Hitler had allowed events to take their course as Jewish businesses were destroyed by rampaging troops and criminal elements of the population. Jews were subjugated as second-class citizens within Germany. More repressive restrictions were placed upon them, as they were blamed for every sort of uprising. With each passing law, anti-Semitism became more prominent. Many Jews were forced to emigrate—luminaries such as Albert Einstein among them.

Hitler was surprised when Britain and France declared war on Germany. His reaction is a mystery, given that he received several warnings prior to September of 1939. Perhaps it can be attributed to their noncommittal stance regarding Hitler's previous annexations. Or perhaps he believed that he could enforce his will yet one more time. We have all heard that hindsight is always better than foresight. What if Hitler had not invaded Poland? Would Germany today have the territory it had at the end of August of 1939? Would Hitler have gone down in history as the greatest German to rule his adopted homeland? He had brought Germany out of its greatest shame and defeat: the impositions that the Treaty of Versailles had placed upon a broken nation. Germany's previously broken economy was unrecognizable in 1939. The Autobahn and the Volkswagen were common words in the German vocabulary. Hitler had achieved great things, and Germans felt that they had reached their zenith of glory. Hitler was even portrayed as the "Teutonic Knight" of legendary times. All had seemed glorious, and it was announced that the Third Reich would last a thousand years.

All in Germany seemed well and good. We are reminded, however, of the legacy of destruction. Like a lurking shadow that does not go away, it is stubborn, and it started when Hitler was a boy. The swastika in the archway of the monastery had become too entrenched in a monster's mentality. But speculation cannot change history, and it was already too late for any miraculous intervention. The evil wrought against the Jews and other ethnic groups would manifest completely throughout World War II, and the effects remain even today.

The annihilation of Poland was complete in a mere six weeks. The Poles resisted fiercely, but they were no match for the German army. Hitler was undoubtedly buoyed by his success. He used his underlings to carry out his most destructive policies. He delegated the job of eliminating the Polish aristocracy to his loyal henchmen, Reinhard Heydrich and Heinrich Himmler. Both were proficient in completing the brutal task, as 90 percent were executed. The Polish Jews were summarily rounded up and annihilated throughout Warsaw's ghettos. Only a scant few survived to tell the horrific account of Nazi atrocities.

During the early part of World War II, Hitler signed a secret directive that ordered German doctors to eliminate persons who were found mentally incompetent or were diagnosed with sickness and disease. Ostensibly, his decree was meant to accord them a merciful death. It was to be the foundation of Hitler's legacy: the establishment of more concentration camps and the eradication of millions of Jews and Gypsies. Other races and nationalities did not escape obliteration either.

The term *blitzkrieg* would become a household word. *Webster's New World Dictionary* defines *blitzkrieg* as "sudden, swift large-scale offensive warfare intended to win a quick victory." Hitler's blitzkrieg saw one nation after another succumb to its effects. Although it was successful, Hitler suffered delusions of grandeur. In Robert Payne's book, *The Life and Death of Adolf Hitler*, Hitler's fantasy was pronounced when he declared: "The German people today are united as one man and I have the support of every German" (p. 378). The German people were against the war. It is a common misconception that Hitler had their complete support.

In 1940 Norway, Denmark, the Netherlands, and Belgium all fell to Hitler's onslaught. In each country, resisters were rounded up and shot. The Jewish populations were sent to area concentration camps. Millions of humans were processed for financial gain. Hitler's tyranny produced human skin for lamps, gold from extracted teeth, and human subjects for grotesque experiments. In the suffocating darkness, few found hope. One Jewish girl from the Netherlands by the name of Anne Frank chronicled a diary that stated her optimistic belief in the goodness of humanity. When the Nazi army invaded Holland, they searched for Jews among the population. Along with most of her family, Anne was discovered in a hidden room behind a bookcase and was sent to a concentration camp. Her diary of hope remains her legacy. Anne died just before her camp was liberated in 1945.

The fall of France was next in line. Hitler entered a half-deserted Paris in 1940. An armistice had been negotiated and signed in June on the same railroad car that had been used for Germany's surrender in 1918. It is certain that Hitler felt vindicated. To him, the former German empire's long humiliation was over. The armistice divided France into two sections; the southern half was governed by French who were loyal to Germany, and the north was administrated by direct German rule. Upon French capitulation, Hitler was the undisputed master of the majority of Europe. Hitler's complete domination of Europe allowed him to conduct his ethnic cleansing agenda on an even greater scale. It became known as the infamous "Final Solution."

Drama surrounded the events of World War II. Rudolph Hess, Hitler's highest-ranking officer and confidant, flew to England in order to procure a peace settlement. Hess was jailed and later sentenced to life in prison at the trials held in Nuremburg in 1945. Many thought Hess was mentally insane. But was it insanity, or was it blind devotion to a tyrannical leader? Another dramatic highlight took place when Hitler broke the Soviet-German Non-Aggression Treaty of 1939. Hitler opened up a second warfront when he attacked the Soviet Union. It was given the code name "Operation Barbarossa." Over three million German soldiers were deployed and captured whole units of Soviet soldiers. Hitler's downfall was in not having heeded illustrations shown throughout history. The Russian winters were brutal. Had he not learned the lessons of Napoleon?

Attempts upon the life of Hitler resulted in the deaths of many. Some were guilty and were summarily executed. Others were implicated, even though there was no proof of direct involvement. Hitler was at a secret military compound called the Wolf's Lair when a bomb exploded, killing many in attendance. Miraculously, Hitler escaped and was injured only slightly. This event perpetuated the myth that Hitler was divinely protected and was meant to establish the rule of the Third Reich for a thousand years. General Erwin Rommel was Hitler's greatest general. Known as the Desert Fox, he was discovered to be a coconspirator in another assassination attempt on Hitler's life. Hitler gave him the choice of committing suicide and receiving a state funeral, or a public trial and execution. For the honor of his family, Rommel committed suicide.

The United States entered the war when the Japanese empire attacked the naval base at Pearl Harbor in 1941. Japan, Italy, and Germany were allied together and formed what was known as the Axis Powers. Hitler declared war on the United States. The entry of the United States into the war was destined to hasten the demise of Hitler's empire. With its entry onto the world stage, armaments, materials, and soldiers arrived to defeat Hitler's war juggernaut.

As the war neared its end, Hitler became more delusional and preoccupied with the rebuilding of Berlin. Despite his policies of destruction, he sought to preserve the German capitol. He desired to build and restore all that was under his control. Instead, Hitler separated families, destroyed ethnic groups, murdered millions, and left a legacy that will not be easily forgotten. He died in a bunker in the center of his city, Berlin, in April of 1945.

Hitler had been raised as a Catholic. His patterns of destructiveness were not developed overnight. Was there anything that remained of his upbringing by the time he committed suicide in 1945? Could one with such a destructive life be a candidate for redemption? Did he feel any private remorse over the millions who were sent to their deaths as a direct result of his beliefs? Did he take responsibility for causing their deaths?

Adolf Hitler had to have known what he was doing. Millions of lives were destroyed because of him. His legacy is justly attributed as a destructive one. He produced no benefit to humanity. His was a legacy formed by an insatiable lust for power. It remains in the column with despots such as Attila the Hun, Joseph Stalin, and Saddam Hussein.

9

George Washington: A Legacy of Leadership

We have seen what an irresponsible man is capable of when he is allowed the reigns to unfettered leadership. Adolf Hitler was given such leadership, but it can be argued that he did not possess the qualities of a true leader—or at least a benevolent one. Hitler's face has not graced any modern monuments, nor has it been depicted on any world currency, save that whose countries he occupied. Even his descendants changed their last name, fearing the scorn of humanity. When a leader is given the task of guiding and directing responsibly, it must remain his duty to build a legacy that testifies to such qualities and character. His followers then depict him as a figure in history to be revered, not despised.

George Washington was a leader to be revered. It is said that he was a God-fearing man, placing the will of the Almighty above his own concerns. This is a stark dichotomy to those who abused their positions of trust, or those who were unable to show the way as virtuous leaders. Washington had within him an instinctive quality that directed his motives and character. His character, in turn, proved impeccable in serving the soldiers he led and the country he helped to found. His was a legacy of leadership grounded in moral conviction. He is depicted, not only in the United States but throughout the nations of the world, as a leader of integrity. Stamps, coins, monuments, cities, and streets all bear the name of Washington. He is the only president whose name graces one of the fifty states of the United States of America.

In David C. Whitney's book, *The American Presidents*, we are able to glean what was important to George Washington. In May of 1797, Washington wrote of his impending retirement: "If ... I could now and then meet the friends I esteem, it would fill the measure and add zest to my enjoyments; but, if ever this happens, it must be under my own vine and fig tree" (p. 15). As great a man as Washington came to be, home and family were the delights of his life. It is a testament to the character and nature that made up his being. Washington had his priorities in order, and that made for an excellent leader. His stewardship was not dictated by greed, avarice, or any yearning for power.

George Washington was born in Wakefield on Pope's Creek Farm in Westmoreland County, Virginia, in 1732. The Old Style Calendar had his birthday listed as February 11, but it is recognized on our current calendars as February 22. He was raised near present day Mount Vernon, his eventual home and estate. Washington's parents, Augustine and Mary Ball Washington, were owners of a vast estate of ten thousand acres of farmland, and several slaves. Upon the death of his father, George's older brother Lawrence inherited most of the property of Mount Vernon. George received what was known as Ferry Farm when he turned twenty-one. George's widowed mother, Mary Ball Washington, guided George in what was important in life. She played a crucial role in his upbringing, instilling within him the virtues that he was widely known and appreciated for: honesty, integrity, and civility.

George Washington's character attributes were grounded while he was a young boy in school. His learning was guided by the principles found in regulations called, "Rules of Civility and Decent Behavior in Company and Conversation." These were some of the most important values that he would carry with him throughout his life. They forbade the use of swearing and fostered respect toward every individual. Although Washington was not considered a scholar, his qualities in character far outweighed whatever he lacked in education.

Washington learned the trades and skills of a woodsman and surveyor. He also became proficient at mapmaking. He gained a job surveying the land of one of Virginia's largest landowners, Lord Fairfax, who was related to his brother's wife. In 1754 Washington inherited the large estate of Mount Vernon (which was located nearby) when his brother Lawrence and niece Sarah Washington died within two years of one another.

Washington's talent served him well when he joined the Virginia militia. Washington was appointed as an adjutant, a position his brother Lawrence had held. He was later promoted to lieutenant colonel and faced his first battle in Pennsylvania. He then traveled to Lake Erie as a messenger and informed the French that they were to evacuate their post, Fort Le Boeuf. He eventually engaged in battle against the French in what was known as the French and Indian War. A particular miracle occurred when Washington was fired upon from every direction. He was later credited with having the favor of heaven.

During that same battle, Washington survived four bullets that had lodged into his jacket, even while having two horses shot out from under him. And although Washington lost several confrontations, he was nevertheless promoted by Governor Dinwiddie of Virginia to the rank of colonel over the Virginia militia.

George Washington married Martha Dandridge Custis on January 6, 1759. Martha was the wealthiest woman in Virginia, and being a widow, she had two children from her previous marriage. Although George and Martha had no children of their own, their marriage was a happy one, lasting until George Washington's death in December of 1799. Martha proved a valuable support for George's military and political career. In addition to having wealth, Martha also owned a vast amount of land in Virginia. It was added to several purchases of land that George had already acquired prior to their marriage.

Washington was elected to the local governing body of Virginia, the Virginia House of Burgesses, in 1758. Washington was reelected several times, advancing in valuable experience toward the art of governing. During his time in Virginia, he focused on farming, one of his favorite pastimes. He also concentrated on the development of breeding livestock and growing new crops. Farming and agriculture in general provided an outlet for Washington's public life. George and Martha Washington's social life involved dancing, games, and other sports at Mount Vernon. After Washington became president of the newly formed United States, he often expressed his wish and intention to return to Virginia and Mount Vernon.

The British increase of taxes became unbearable to the colonists, making protest inevitable. Tension between the governors of the colonies and their representatives intensified. In 1769 the governor of Virginia disbanded the House of Burgesses as a result of their dissension over the British Stamp Act. Washington prophetically saw the use of arms as the only way to freedom.

The Stamp Act was enacted by the British as a way to pay for the French and Indian War. In Boston, the colonists rebelled by dumping British tea into their harbor. It became known as the Boston Tea Party. A colonial army was raised, and in 1775 George Washington was chosen as the commander in chief. Washington's preeminence was recognized in his abilities as a military commander and in the leadership traits that had been instilled within him early on.

One does not become a leader immediately but develops as one over a period of time. In *The Making of a Leader*, author Frank Damazio writes, "The great importance of preparation is stamped indelibly in the very fiber of three areas: nature, craftsmanship and Scripture" (p. 129). Inherent within Washington were the fibers of all three. As we have seen, he applied himself to the areas of craftsmanship and nature by virtue of his self-discipline in school and work. Washington's adherence to Scripture was prevalent throughout his life. In his article, "The Federalist Brief," author Marc Arkin quotes from Washington's private prayer book: "O most glorious God ... direct my thoughts, words and work ... daily frame me more into the likeness of thy Son Jesus Christ" (www.earstohear.net).

Arkin also quotes Washington from his farewell address to the nation: "The Foundation of a great Empire is laid, and I please myself with a persuasion, that Providence will not leave its work imperfect." We can therefore see the fabric that was woven through Washington and his character. The foundation of God in his life proved the success of George Washington. He was quick to recognize the Lord's hand upon the building of a new nation, and the Lord's providential placement in having Washington as a part of it. We see his adherence to Scripture as found in Proverbs 16:3 (KJV): "Commit thy works unto the Lord, and thy thoughts shall be established." It can be said, therefore, that Washington's thoughts upon the Lord established him as a great leader.

The Revolutionary War began with the signing of the Declaration of Independence. In it the signers pledged their very lives, acknowledging that what they had gained was endowed by their Creator. When the colonies declared their independence from Britain in 1776, many sacrificed their homes, livestock, and wealth to birth a new nation. George Washington was no different. He forfeited whatever he could and gave everything for the cause. His humility was another great secret to his success as an extraordinarily great leader.

It is part of his legacy that he refused to accept any pay as commander in chief of the Continental Army. He asked only for the repayment of his expenses. It was a generous offer to a newly formed Congress that was financially strapped and could ill afford any expense whatsoever.

In October of 1781, George Washington led a victorious but weary, ragtag army to accept the surrender of the British general, Lord Cornwallis. It marked a defining point for Washington and ended the Revolutionary War. Independence was secured. Washington, who had faced insurmountable obstacles in achieving triumph, was hailed as a true leader. He was seen as one who had overcome multiple barriers. His goal completed, he looked again to retiring at Mount Vernon.

Washington's contribution to the new military defined his legacy in leadership. He had established the preeminence of civilian authority when he deferred to the new Continental Congress during the war. Additionally, the role of the citizen soldier was enhanced by Washington's use of the "minute man." The minute man was the individual farmer or ordinary citizen who was called upon on short notice to fill the needs of the military. Moreover, Washington established the character of the armed forces by lending it his own example of high ethical standards. Washington's physical and moral courage further contributed to stabilizing the military and the new country as a whole.

In 1787 Washington was called again to the service of his country, as he presided over the Constitutional Convention held in Philadelphia. His presence was critical to its success. He contributed to the new political structure by providing leadership in drafting a constitution. As a result, the new United States Constitution was ratified by the thirteen original states the following year and was enacted in 1789.

In February of 1789, Washington became the first president of the United States. His excellent leadership, and the abilities that accompanied it, were compelling enough reasons for the first electoral college to vote for him. Washington was known for not having abused his position as commander in chief of the Continental Army. Additionally, his honesty and integrity were legendary.

Washington set examples and customs that have been followed by his successors. He ended the first inaugural address with the words "So help me God" while placing his hand upon the Bible. Washington provided further leadership when he asked the new Congress to enact the Bill of Rights. He established the presidential veto in April of 1792 and the cabinet system that is in use today. During his second term in office, Washington set another tradition by refusing to run for another four years.

Washington's legacy of leadership was furthered by his sense of duty to God and to his country. He relied on God's power to guide his own destiny, as well as that of the new nation. As we have seen, he exemplified perseverance and loyalty in the face of adversity. When the new government was formed, he extended those same qualities to both individuals and the new institutions that were needed.

Washington's vision provided direction for the country and for those who served it. He demonstrated that he had great insight into the capabilities of his fellow countrymen and a deeper understanding of the events that unfolded around him. George Washington's legacy of leadership has benefited humanity ever since. Washington died in December of 1799, leaving his country in deep mourning.

10

Jesus Christ: The Greatest Legacy of All

We have traveled the vast expanse of history and have viewed legacies of every kind. Those who left a legacy that benefited humanity are remembered as timeless patrons of good, while those that were bent on evil and destruction are committed to memory as despicable tyrants and despots. Others, such as Czar Nicholas II and the Jesus' disciple Thomas, were in need of a more defined focus, thereby causing a realignment of the legacy that was otherwise left intact. Some legacies are not as black-and-white as others. Many have remained in the field of discussion for years, and analysts remain mystified as to where they need to be assigned.

Although a legacy is likely to take several twists and turns, it is judged by the benefits the individual left behind. We have seen the overriding good that George Washington left. William Wallace, a type of George Washington, became the symbol of Scottish independence. He was the younger son of a minor nobleman, without power, privilege, or patronage. He rose to become a leader while barely out of his teen years. His legacy was established, along with a desire at an early age to fulfill his purpose in freeing his countrymen from tyrannical rule. Peter the Great, considered one of Russia's greatest czars, discovered his purpose by barely surviving a siege at the Kremlin as a young man. He watched as many of his family and relatives were slaughtered by rebellious boyars. He had an indication of what his legacy would be. It was formed by events that would carry his name into the future.

We have, as the saying goes, saved the best for last. This person needs no assignment of his legacy to those who are His followers. They know where He has stood and why He continues to astonish those who are living still. His legacy has impacted humanity throughout the centuries. Men have lived and died for His cause. He knew and possessed, as one who belonged in the lineage of royalty, an inner expectation and understanding of what was expected of Him. He has left a great deal that has changed the world forever. His is undoubtedly the greatest of all legacies. That legacy belongs to Jesus Christ.

We must delve into the life of Jesus Christ to establish His legacy further. Such an investigation can ascertain facts that are needed to make the claim that His was and is the greatest of all legacies. We must also look into His purpose. He claimed to have a plan for humanity. What was it, and why would He give His life for such a plan? Additionally, it is important to discover some of the aspects as to why He was considered a figure with such impact. The Word of God has referred to Him as the "Wonderful Counselor." Why was such a characteristic given to Him? He has been attributed many names: healer, dayspring, bright and morning star, the Anointed One, and Messiah, to name a few. Why was His legacy greater than all of those that we have mentioned thus far? Believers in Christ as the Savior, the Son of God, can clearly understand why, but what of those who do not believe? How do we convince them? What must we show them? How was Jesus so different from George Washington, Caesar Augustus, or Dr. Martin Luther King? Were they not good men with good intentions?

The purpose of Christ can be seen as the first level of foundation that created His legacy. In Mel Gibson's book, *The Passion*, he quotes Scripture out of Isaiah 53:7: "And he was led as a lamb to the slaughter. And as a sheep is silent before the shearers, he did not open his mouth" (p. 64). Mel further states in his forward, "My hope is that *The Passion of the Christ* will help many more people recognize the power of His love and let Him help them to save their own lives." Here, we can see the beginning and purpose of the reason Jesus came: to suffer, to die, and to bring the love of God to many in dramatic fashion in order that humanity might be saved. Jesus came to reconcile humanity to God, and God to humanity. Through His death, He became a bridge of reconciliation.

We further see His purpose clarified in Isaiah 53:11 (NIV): "After the suffering of his soul, he will see the light of life and be satisfied; by his knowledge my righteous servant will justify many, and he will bear their iniquities." The book of Isaiah shows that Jesus knew why He came, and that knowledge solidified His purpose. Jesus was motivated in His willingness to fulfill the Father's will to become a sacrifice for sin. He understood why He had come and that

He was anointed, appointed, and empowered by His Father to fulfill His purpose and destiny. His surety of such created a foundation for His own legacy and for those who would seek their own destiny and purpose. Isaiah's statements were remarkable, in that they were written as prophecies several hundred years before the time of Jesus Christ. Christ therefore fulfilled His purpose prophetically.

Knowing why Jesus came piques our curiosity as to the furtherance of His purpose. In J. Dwight Pentecost's book, *The Words and Works of Jesus Christ, a Study of the Life of Christ*, he states, "The apostles were eyewitnesses and servants of the Word. They were commissioned to go into all the world and preach the Gospel" (p. 27). In *Webster's New World Dictionary*, the word *commission* is defined as "an authorization to perform certain duties, tasks, or to take on certain powers or that which a person is authorized to do for another."

One can see clear evidence that another purpose found in Jesus Christ's life was to pass on the authorization to proliferate, or spread, his message, the gospel. A person's legacy remains intact when followers carry it onward. *Webster's* defines the word *purpose* as "to intend, plan, or resolve with determination." Therefore, one can conclude that Jesus clearly intended to pass on His plans and authorization to fulfill His purpose, through His disciples (as we have seen in Thomas) and through those who would follow Him.

Knowing that His purpose would have to continue even after His death, it was important to Jesus to commission His apostles, even as it is important for us to commission others in today's world. J. Dwight Pentecost further states in *The Words and Works of Jesus Christ*: "This truth concerning Jesus Christ was formalized and passed from the apostles to succeeding generations" (p. 27). Thus far, we have seen the reasons for which Jesus came and why it was important for humanity to know. It is equally important to note the methods Jesus used to carry out His purpose, thereby leaving His legacy.

In studying the life of Jesus Christ and reviewing His methods, we learn our own purpose as Christians. In Ted Haggard's book, *Primary Purpose*, he makes the following comment: "Jesus encourages us not to enter into personal conflict or argument over temporal issues. Our hearts can't handle it" (p. 120). Jesus stayed on track with His vision and purpose when He remained focused on His reason for coming to earth. He served His Father, the house of Israel, and humanity by staying focused on the kingdom of God. This empowered Him to be used by the Holy Spirit continuously.

Jesus also knew that He was empowered by the Holy Spirit with gifts to bring His Father glory. The exhibition of these gifts made it evident that it was His purpose to show God's love, power, and glory. The demonstration of miracles, healings, and discerning of spirits strengthened His purpose and legacy. He poured out His life in order to show us that this same method would confirm our own purpose.

Jesus understood the destiny that was placed upon His life. Acts 10:38 (NIV) states, "God anointed Jesus with the Holy Spirit and power, and how he went around doing good and healing all who were under the power of the devil, because God was with him." With a clear focus and a sharp vision of fulfilling the Father's will, Jesus had everything necessary to further His purpose. It was God's anointing upon Jesus that helped Him to carry out His mission, just as we have seen in the case of King David.

In Kenneth E. Hagin's book, *A Fresh Anointing*, he states the following: "Thirty years after Jesus' birth, we see that he was anointed with the Holy Spirit. He was endued with power from on High; anointed with the Holy Spirit to carry out his ministry on earth" (p. 10). Although Jesus knew his position as the Son of God, He was also anointed from heaven for service to carry out His purpose. When Jesus was anointed, He also returned with power. He knew that it took the power and anointing of the Holy Spirit to complete His purpose.

We must interject that this alone separated Him from all the legacies that we have mentioned so far. Although King David was anointed, Jesus operated in miracles and the power of the Holy Spirit. Jesus read from the book of Isaiah, as noted in Luke 4:18 (KJV): "The Spirit of the Lord is upon me, because he hath anointed me." His recognition that He was anointed empowered Him to operate with the gifts of the Holy Spirit. His confidence came from His Father and from the fact that He knew the Holy Spirit had empowered him.

We know that a policeman is recognized by his uniform or his badge. His identification is further evidence that he is authorized to carry out the duties of his office. In this capacity, he bears many names: officer, policeman, or law official. As Jesus was identified through the fulfillment of prophecy and the gifts of the Holy Spirit, He was also recognized by the many names He bore. He is known as the Prince of Peace, the mighty God, the bishop of souls, Chief Shepherd, and the Word of Life.

Additionally, he has been referred to as the "faithful and true witness," "Christ, our life," and "wonderful counselor."

We know that Jesus is the common denominator that binds all the monikers attached to Him. Matthew 1:23 (KJV) says, "Behold, a virgin shall be with child, and shall bring forth a Son, and they shall call his name Immanuel, which being interpreted is, God with us." It is certain that this pointed to Jesus' purpose: God being among us in the form of his Son, Jesus.

Jesus Christ also has the only legacy that has manifested itself in a tangible way. Through His namesake, and by evidence of the Holy Spirit whom He sent to us upon His ascension, we know that His life in us is what gives life itself. A legacy that has a living testimony is powerful indeed, and one that leaves several names can be seen as incomparable. All of the names mentioned, however, have pointed to one name that exemplifies and glorifies Him altogether.

In T. C. Horton's book, *The Names of Christ*, he points out the following: "How rarely do we bow together to seek that heavenly wisdom, that divine counsel, which alone will enable us to find our way?" (p. 32). As mentioned previously, Jesus is referred to as the "bishop of souls" and the Chief Shepherd. It is widely known that a shepherd watches over his sheep, carefully guarding his prized possessions, tending to all their needs and seeing that they are kept out of danger. As the bishop of souls, Jesus is the caretaker who leads, comforts, and guides.

There have been many names attributed to Jesus Christ, but "wonderful counselor" is the one name that exemplifies the God He embodied. Isaiah 9:6 (RV) states, "Unto us a child is born, unto us a son is given: and the government shall be upon his shoulder: and His name shall be called Wonderful Counselor, The Mighty God, The Everlasting Father, The Prince of Peace." It is noteworthy that Jesus is mentioned first as the wonderful counselor. It is the name that serves as a chord that binds all the others.

In Jerome Rodale's tome, *The Synonym Finder*, the word *counselor* has numerous attachments. A counselor is also known as an advisor, mentor, teacher, leader, guide, and tutor. Additionally, the word *counsel* is attributed the following assignments: instruction, guidance, direction, and teaching. *Webster's New World Dictionary, Second College Edition* defines *counselor* as "one who advises" while defining *counsel* as "to urge the acceptance of action" or "to give wisdom and judgment."

Nowhere is this better illustrated than in the account of Jesus' teaching in the temple as a young boy in the midst of the teachers. Luke 2:46–48 (NKJV) states it beautifully: "And they found Him in the temple, both listening to them and asking them questions. And all who heard Him were astonished as His understanding and answers. So when they saw Him, they were amazed." It is noteworthy that Jesus, at such a young age, was already displaying several characteristics of an excellent counselor: namely, one who listens, one who asks questions, and one who displays wisdom and judgment.

In Hebrews 4:15 (NIV), the following passage comes to light: "For we do not have a high priest who is unable to sympathize with our weaknesses, but we have one who has been tempted in every way, just as we are, yet, was without sin." Because Jesus Christ now serves as our high priest, and has experienced human temptation, how much more does He stand ready to give immediate and sympathetic help when we are tempted? Considering His example of one who has partaken of the human condition, we should be all the more ready to embrace His counsel in our every situation and time of need. As part of His legacy, Jesus left us an example of the best strategy for overcoming any trial we may face. In every situation He was confronted with, He overcame by looking to His Father for the guidance He needed.

Although Jesus never overlooked sin, He understood sinners and always showed kindness and respect to those who were willing to learn, repent, and change their behavior. In William Barclay's book, *Jesus as They Saw Him*, he writes, "The name of Jesus underlines the real humanity of our Lord. In New Testament times it was one of the commonest of names" (p. 10). It was through that very essence of humanity that Jesus was able to minister hope, healing, and life to the multitudes that sought Him. It is another layer and foundation added to the legacy of Christ that His concern and example went beyond the time frame of His own day and age. Jesus provided the example needed to continue to benefit humanity with a vision that extended worldwide.

Additionally, Jesus possessed personality traits that provided a further example for us and displayed once again His attributes as the "wonderful counselor." Jesus was always honest, compassionate, and sensitive. He never lost sight of the fact that He was committed to serving His Father and His fellow man while on earth. Jesus also prepared and applied himself in ministry through prayer and meditation. As He knew the Word, He caused others to think and act correctly according to godly principles.

Another foundation of the legacy of Jesus Christ can be found in the many miracles and healings attributed to Him. Jesus was always attuned to the situation at hand. In Gordon Lindsay's book, *The Life and Teachings of Christ*, he noted, "One of the mistakes of some who minister healing is that they often fail to give their listeners proper instructions. Jesus, however, in His perfect understanding of the human heart, always went directly to the seat of trouble" (p. 208). A wonderful illustration of this is found in Luke 11:24–26 (NIV). After casting a demon out of a man who was mute, Jesus warned those who were listening, "When an evil spirit comes out of a man, it goes through arid places seeking rest and does not find it. Then it says, 'I will return to the house I left.' When he finds the house clean, it brings seven more spirits more wickedly than itself. And the final condition of that man is worse than the first." Jesus never overlooked an urgent situation. When an opportunity arose for healing or a miracle to take place, it was part of Jesus' legacy that He left further instructions to benefit His listeners' lives.

It is interesting to note that Jesus made another statement immediately following this dramatic turn of events. It was important to Him that everyone listening would remember not only what took place but the lesson behind it. In Luke 11:28 (NIV), Jesus instructed his listeners, "Blessed are those who hear the Word of God and obey it." He left instructions for those who were healed and for those who were listening. He preceded His instructions with a warning as to what would happen should the recipient of His miracle not follow His implicit counsel. Even through His many displays of miracles and healings, Jesus continued to look at the hearts of those involved.

In Craig Hill's book, *The Ancient Paths*, he writes, "In whatever area our identity has been cursed in the past, fear will potentially motivate us to idolatry. Then you are looking to someone or something other than Jesus Christ as the source of our life" (p. 105). This statement is epitomized in the Samaritan woman at the well as seen in John 4:10–19. Although the woman had found her identity in her past relationships with many men, which indicated skewed motives, Jesus nevertheless reached out to her with honesty and compassion. In turn, the woman experienced a miracle in her heart and a healing that caused her to bring the message of hope and salvation back to her own village. The woman set her eyes upon Jesus rather than her own circumstances. Instead of taking a judgmental stand, Jesus listened and applied the truth to her condition. Jesus was sympathetic to the human need and condition. He understood the heart, as He was the creator of it.

In His time, Jesus dealt with many of the same issues we see in the modern age. He dealt with problems that people today deal with: anxiety, loneliness, marriage problems, fear, sex, and pride. Comparisons can be made by his followers; in particular, his disciples. When Jesus stated that the time was approaching for Him to die, His disciples were full of fear, anxiety, and loneliness. Jesus continued His example and provided the comfort and reassurance they needed. When the disciples were full of fear and anxiety during the raging storm around them, Jesus calmly stood in the midst of the sea and cried out, "Peace, be still!" Jesus remains the best of all examples when we are faced with uncertainty.

Jesus served as the best example and counselor in every circumstance. This causes us to remember that we are merely His agents doing His work. As such, we represent His ministry here on earth. In J. Dwight Pentecost's book, *The Words and Works of Jesus Christ*, he states, "The twelve disciples might have anticipated that as a result of their ministry they would receive the same public acclaim that Jesus was receiving as a result of His ministry, but such was not to be. In view of such warnings that they would be persecuted, Christ gave a number of encouragements" (p. 195). Jesus gave warnings without hesitation, but He always coupled them with words of encouragement and comfort. Another aspect was demonstrated when Jesus instructed the young rich man to give all that he had to the poor. As seen in Luke 18:23, the man stated to Jesus that he had followed the law all of his life. He became very sad upon hearing what Jesus wanted him to do, as he was a man of great wealth.

It is part of Jesus' legacy that He looked straight at the heart and addressed what was needed to resolve any issue. In Jesus' day, people's problems were evident: they wanted attention or sympathy, and they held on to whatever gave them security. Some problems provided benefits that people did not want to give up. In the case of the young rich man,

Jesus knew that his heart and security were attached to his wealth. Jesus brought this to his attention to let him know that he was responsible for any improvement needed in his life.

Thus far, we have chosen to focus upon the name of Christ as "wonderful counselor." We have explained some of the reasons that this name was given to Him. But what are we to say to convince the nonbeliever that Jesus was the Son of God? The many names given to Christ must be reflected through the redemptive work of the cross. It has remained, throughout the centuries, the centerpiece and legacy of what Christ was all about, and it explains, once and for all, who He was. It was Peter who declared, "Thou art the Son of the Most High God!"

Jesus Christ acknowledged Himself as the Son of God. No other adherent or founder of a religion has claimed this except Jesus. We must, however, look at another aspect of the legacy of Jesus Christ that continues to resonate even today. When we are reminded of what Louis XIV left, it is encapsulated in the restored structure of Versailles. When we think of Caesar Augustus, we picture the ruins of ancient Rome. But it remains the redemptive work of the cross through which Jesus Christ left a living legacy of healing that continues today. The work wrought through the cross has caused millions to be healed and saved worldwide.

The legacy of Jesus Christ is further enhanced by the fact that He provided for the fulfillment of God's promises for health and healing. As man has relentlessly devised remedies to postpone his eventual demise, he has failed to grasp fully what Jesus Christ accomplished on the cross of Cavalry. Man has sought his own way to put off his eventual demise. Tribes of the Caucasus Mountains of Russia have sworn that their longevity is a result of simple eating and arduous work. The famous "snake oil" remedies of the Wild West and the miracle waters of Lourdes, France, have promised healing. Across the Asian plateau, people of oriental culture have devised herbal concoctions and meditation as a way of adding years to life. Invariably, every culture, tribe, and race has sought to strengthen their health and increase their longevity through their own methods and devices.

We must look further into what Jesus accomplished, by discovering what He left for us: promises that bring health and healing to those who follow Him. In turn, health and healing introduce us to His greatest promise: eternal life. When Jesus spoke to the masses throughout Israel, he spread the message of His free gift of eternal life, and He demonstrated God's love through miracles and healings. We must also recognize that the covenant established through Jesus Christ laid a foundation for these promises. His life, which ended upon the cross, laid the groundwork and confirmed that healing is for all—and that God still performs His healing miracles in the world today. His legacy would not be complete without a review of these things.

Children at play will sometimes make a promise through a "blood covenant" pact. Inevitably, they seal that promise by cutting a finger to "mingle the blood." Promises can be made with childlike fantasy or with a note of seriousness between nations, politicians, or groups of people. Here, a greater definition is needed, as promises include an element of trust. The word *promise* is defined in the *New Merriam-Webster Dictionary* as "ground for expectation of success of improvement."

The promises that Jesus fulfilled upon His death on the cross were grounds for the expectation of success or improvement. Indeed, His resurrection ushered in the promise of eternal life as well as the promise of health and healing. God's standards and promises form a bedrock from which to launch our belief for a miracle or healing. Psalm 37:4 (RSV) states, "Delight in the Lord and He will give you the desires of your heart." Who can argue with the fact that it is everyone's desire to be in good health and to be healed? It is credited to the legacy of Christ that the Word states that all were healed who came to Him.

One who is sick desires to be well. In F. F. Bosworth's *Christ the Healer*, he notes, "It is only to the obedient, those who will 'diligently hearken to the voice of the Lord and do that which is right in His sight,' that it is said, 'The Lord will take away from you all sickness'" (p. 37). It was Jesus' desire to heal all those who came to Him. Numerous stories throughout Scripture have testified to His compassion and ability to heal many from infirmities of all kinds.

Healing is a promise straight from the authority of God's Word, established by the work that Jesus completed upon His death on the cross. We see further in Deuteronomy 7:15 (RSV) that same promise: "And the Lord will take away from you all sickness; and none of the evil diseases of Egypt, which you knew, will He inflict upon you." It is noteworthy that Exodus 15:26 adds a clause that became a name for God: "I am the Lord, who heals you." In the Hebrew language He was called Yahweh Rapha, or "God, the healer." In Philip Gehlhar's book, *Healing from Cancer and All Other Diseases*, he points out, "When people asked God for healing, He did not refuse" (p. 39). Gehlhar writes further, "Even a Syrian officer, Namaan, sought Elisha the prophet to heal him of leprosy" (2 Kings 5:1–15). Hezekiah prayed and God added fifteen years to his life (2 Kings 20:1–8). Another King, Asa, did not seek help from the Lord, only from the doctors. He remained infirm in his feet until he died (2 Chronicles 16:12)" (p. 39). The Word of God is filled with promises. They are understood fully when the covenant of Abraham and Christ are understood. Theirs was a covenant of blood, one that was binding forever.

Another promise is found in James 5:14–16 (RSV): "Is any sick among you? Let him call for the elders of the church; and let him pray over him, anointing him with oil in the name of the lord; and the prayer of the faith shall save the sick." We can see that as the promises of God are established, the promises fulfilled through Jesus Christ become more of a reality. Again, it is His legacy that healing remains available to all who ask for it.

In Marilyn Hickey's book, *Be Healed*, she states the following: "Faith produces great results because the power to heal is released" (p. 52). God promises that "the prayer of faith shall save the sick." In Dr. Fred Price's book, *Is Healing for All?*, he makes the following statement: "Peter came to realize and know about Jesus' attitude concerning sickness and disease" (p. 91). We can see Peter's statement reflecting his viewpoint and observations in the book of Acts. In Acts

10:38 (RSV) he states, "How God anointed Jesus of Nazareth with the Holy Ghost and with power; who went about doing good and healing all." Jesus stated that He and the Father were one. It was God's will to heal all, and it remains so today. His promise to heal can therefore be enacted through faith and anointing, such as that which was placed upon Jesus. The Word of God states that even as He was crucified upon the cross, many were healed. None of the legacies we have mentioned so far—or could ever name—could claim to have healed the sick upon their deathbeds.

Hebrews 13:8 (RSV) states, "Jesus Christ is the same yesterday, today and forever." It further declares in verse 12: "Jesus also suffered ... to sanctify the people through his own blood." A definition for *sanctify* and *sanctity* can be expressed as "to be free from sin." When we understand that sin can be a hindrance to healing, we can see that the blood of Jesus conquered sickness and disease. Once again, there is no one but Jesus Christ who bears such a legacy.

Just as animals were used in Old Testament times to atone for the sins of the people, so the blood of Christ was poured out to atone for sin, sickness, and disease. A covenant was established through Jesus when He became the redemptive, sacrificial lamb. Isaiah 53:5 further attests to this fact: "And with his stripes we are healed."

In the book *Promises from God's Word*, Isaiah 53:5 is further expounded upon: "He was wounded for our rebellious acts. He was crushed for our sins. He was punished so that we could have peace, and we received healing from his wounds" (p. 111). Healing was part of God's covenant plan through the sacrifice of Jesus Christ. In the covenant established through Christ, the blood of Jesus cleanses us from sin, rather than just covering it as the old covenant did. Through Jesus and His atonement, God became our helper.

In E. W. Kenyon's book, *The Blood Covenant*, he writes, "The blood of bulls and goats did not cleanse the conscience, did not take away sin consciousness from man" (p. 33). Under the old covenant, it could therefore be argued that a "sin consciousness" could have prevented any sort of belief that it is God's will for all to be healed. A perpetual condition of sin consciousness brought about an unending ritual of sacrifice. Jesus' shedding of His own blood cleansed that consciousness effectively enough to allow His light into the thinking process. Now, because of Jesus and His establishment of the new covenant, healing is not only a thought but a "covenant-established" fact. Jesus was the final sacrifice that was offered, effectively breaking the unending cycle of animal sacrifices.

In Kenneth Hagin's book, *Seven Things You Should Know About Divine Healing*, he emphatically writes, "Jesus actually, literally, took the cause of our sickness and disease ... His sin-bearing was that we might be free from sin, and the object of his sickness-bearing was that we might be free from sickness" (p. 8). We must remind ourselves again that Jesus Christ is the same yesterday, today, and forever. It becomes relevant even more when doubt comes in. Jesus bore our sins, sicknesses, and diseases upon the cross. What He accomplished in the past is just as relevant for today.

Matthew 3:17 (RSV) says it succinctly: "He himself took our infirmities, and bore our sicknesses." This is a powerful statement and a testament to Jesus Christ Himself. He was willing to endure the excruciating pain of a Roman crucifixion, for He knew what awaited Him on the other side of death. Through His endurance, He provided what we needed to receive God's promises for us. Additionally, the legacy of Jesus Christ is a current and active one. Healing has not passed away but continues on because of the redemptive work of the cross.

Because of Christ, nothing about God's plan for healing sickness and disease has changed, although much of the modern church's attitude toward healing has changed. Belief in God's power and desire to work healing miracles has faded in a materialistic society where the greater emphasis has been placed on medical science and wealth. Indeed, there is a tendency today to make doctors into gods of healing.

Other religions have also looked for healing from gods that have done nothing for them. In some parts of the world, people go to witch doctors, who seek spirits to break curses. Some cultures teach meditation and mantras, while the New Age movement has stressed that all healing comes from one's own inner strength and healing power. The idea that Jesus Christ alone can heal has proved to be beyond the reasoning of nonbelievers.

In James Allen's book, *As a Man Thinketh*, he states, "The body is the servant of the mind. Disease and health, like circumstances, are rooted in thought" (p. 33). Healing is as active as the thinking process. Proverbs 17:22 (RSV) states, "A merry heart is like a good medicine." It takes a jovial thought to bring about convulsive laughter. The Word of God states that this is like a good medicine. Healing is a current action that never ceases. Jesus left an active legacy by giving us the opportunity to be healed. This legacy is in sharp contrast to all others.

Jesus gave us His name as a legacy. The Bible refers to it as the "name above all names." Countless Scriptures point to the importance of calling upon the name of Jesus Christ. The apostles commanded healing for people "in the name of Jesus of Nazareth." Jesus Christ is the only one through whom we are able to be healed from sin and disease. Calling upon Him is the first and only step to true healing. Philip Gehlhar's book, *Healing from Cancer and Other Diseases*, states, "We affirm the authority and power of that name of Yahweh Rapha. When we place His name upon us, we affirm His ownership of our bodies and lives" (p. 29).

We have seen the legacy of Jesus established as both a unique and living legacy. However, what we have stated thus far is only a minute part of what He left for us. When people leave a will or testament to be carried out upon the event of their deaths, the estate remains in probate until all legal matters are settled. Before Jesus died, He settled accounts in a unique way. When the disciple John and Jesus' mother, Mary, were standing together at the foot of the cross, Jesus was mindful of Mary's plight. In John 19:26–27 (KJV), He provided for His mother by entrusting her into the care of His disciple John. "When Jesus therefore saw His mother, and the disciple standing by, whom He loved, He saith unto His mother, 'Woman, behold thy son!' Then saith He to the disciple, 'Behold thy mother!' And from that hour that disciple took her unto his own home."

Jesus took great care in finalizing His will upon the cross. According to the gospel of John, His last words are a testament to that very fact. We find this illustrated further in John 19:30 (KJV): "When Jesus therefore had received the vinegar, He said, 'It is finished:' and He bowed His head, and gave up the ghost." The phrase "it is finished," when derived from the Greek word *tetelaesthe*, can be literally defined as something finished that is never to be worked again. Jesus made the startling statement that what He had just done would be done only once, never to be done again. His legacy must be seen a living one. He became the sacrifice needed for the atonement of sin, once and for all. His sacrifice still atones for sin today.

We have stated the need to further establish facts for the benefit of the unbeliever regarding Jesus Christ. Critics, agnostics, and atheists often refuse to believe in the existence of Jesus or to acknowledge His place in history. Their derision can be a result of not recognizing the four Synoptic Gospels as an eyewitness account. In Grant R. Jeffrey's book, *Jesus, the Great Debate*," he writes, "Another critic, Salomon Reinach, contemptuously refuses 'to consider writings founded upon the memory of a collection of illiterates as historical evidence for Jesus'" (p. 160). We must further note that critics such as Reinach would also have to invalidate accounts from eyewitnesses who have written on past historical events or subjects. Josephus, perhaps the most prolific of Jewish historical writers, would have agreed with the gospel accounts, and he was an eyewitness to much of what he wrote.

C. S. Lewis, one of Britain's most well-known atheists, converted to Christianity after having studied all the facts regarding Jesus Christ. After his conversion, he became the Lord's most ardent supporter. Once an opponent of the Savior, he now defended Him vociferously. Grant R. Jeffrey further quotes Lewis: "You must make your choice. Either this man was and is the Son of God: or else a madman or something worse" (p. 29). The teachings of Jesus, along with the miracles He presented, were in contradiction to any claim that he was a madman. Neither could He be labeled as just a good philosopher. C. S. Lewis berated those who debated against him, chiding them for dismissing Jesus as merely a human teacher with good qualities.

We have mentioned that Dr. Martin Luther King Jr. had good qualities and intentions, as did George Washington and Caesar Augustus. Washington and King were believers in Christ. As we have already seen, their actions and deeds were based upon what Christ taught. As powerful as Caesar Augustus may have been, he did not place himself upon a cross to heal humanity, nor did he ascribe to the title of "wonderful counselor." We are reminded that his legacy was laden with self-appointed titles. When comparing such legacies with that of Jesus Christ, His stands alone. Even the emperor of France, Napoleon Bonaparte, acknowledged that Jesus Christ filled the "wants of man."

We must ask ourselves, what of the Gospels? Are they an accurate record and testimony to the life and miracles of Jesus Christ? If so, they also stand as a testimony to the legacy of Christ. It is a fair question when asked by a nonbeliever, and one that deserves an answer from the Scriptures. In Acts 2:22 (KJV), the apostle Luke writes, "Ye men of Israel, hear these words; Jesus of Nazareth, a man approved of God among you by miracles and wonders and signs, which God did by Him in the midst of you." Luke makes the statement that there were many eyewitnesses to what Jesus did. This not only proves the existence and validity of Christ, but it solidifies His legacy as a miracle worker. It is something that neither Mohammed nor Confucius claimed. Additionally, Luke challenged his readers and listeners to analyze what Jesus had done. He did not want them to doubt what had taken place. He wanted to further strengthen the faith of Jesus' followers.

Jesus' legacy is anchored in the accuracy of the Word of God. The Word of God itself is supported by archeological evidence, ancient manuscripts (both Jewish and pagan writings), and prophecies that point to Jesus as the Messiah. The tomb of Caiaphas, the high priest, for example, was discovered in a recent archeological dig, while the Dead Sea scrolls were found by accident. The Shroud of Turin—believed by some to be the genuine burial cloth of Christ, and by others to be an elaborate forgery—has provided fascinating conjecture. Regardless, a wealth of information is available. In every case, discoveries have confirmed or enhanced the Word of God in every detail. As the Word has been authenticated through historical evidence, so has the legacy that Jesus left for us here on earth. On this evidence alone, our basis for establishing the legacy of Jesus Christ is concrete.

It is part of Christ's legacy that He was the fulfillment of hundreds of prophecies written in the Word and in ancient texts. The probability of someone other than Christ having fulfilled them are astronomical. It is important to look at some of these, as they lend credence to our position that Jesus has the greatest of all legacies. The first prophecy mentioned in the Word of God is found in Genesis 3:15 (KJV): "And I will put enmity between thee and the woman, and between thy seed and her seed; it shall bruise thy head, and thou shalt bruise his heel." Passing judgment to the Serpent for having deceived Eve, God spoke prophetically that Jesus would crush the head of Satan.

Scripture records the fulfillment of this particular passage in Revelation 1:18 (KJV), where Jesus proclaimed, "I am He that liveth, and was dead; and, behold, I am alive for evermore, Amen; and have the keys of hell and of death." When Jesus stated that He had the keys of hell and death, He effectively stripped Satan of any authority he may have had. Upon Jesus' death on the cross, He enacted Colossians 2:15: "And having spoiled principalities and powers, He made a show of them openly, triumphing over them in it."

We can see that God's wisdom is hidden and ordained by Him, even enshrouded in prophecy. When God pronounced judgment upon the Serpent, He concealed from Satan the fact that Christ would be the fulfillment of that sentence. This is illustrated in 1 Corinthians 1:7 (KJV): "But we speak the wisdom of God in a mystery, even the hidden wisdom, which God ordained before the world unto our glory." The result of Christ's death on the cross was kept from Satan but was revealed by Christ in His resurrection. Another illustration in 1 Corinthians 1:8 (KJV) shows us the reaction of Satan and his forces: "Which none of the princes of this world knew: for had they known it, they would not have crucified the Lord of glory." Christ's legacy was to fulfill prophecy and to reveal the mysteries of God's wisdom in due course. We must look at additional prophecies as further evidence that Jesus Christ was not merely human but God incarnate, born in the flesh to redeem humanity from his sinful state.

Old Testament prophecies predicted the coming of Jesus as Messiah. Without such a redeemer, we would be left in the mire of our sins. It is the crown of Christ's legacy that He came not only as Messiah but to fulfill that which was written of Him long ago. Isaiah 7:14 (KJV) records another prophecy concerning Christ: "Therefore the Lord Himself shall give you a sign; Behold, a virgin shall conceive, and bear a son, and shall call His name Immanuel." The fulfillment of this prophecy first appears in the New Testament as an announcement to Mary in Luke 1:31: "And behold, thou shalt conceive in thy womb, and bring forth a son, and shall call His name Jesus." The direct fulfillment is then shown in Luke 2:7: "And she brought forth her firstborn son, and wrapped Him in swaddling clothes, and laid Him in a manger." We can see clearly that Jesus was concealed throughout the Old Testament but was revealed in the New Testament.

The coming of the Messiah was established through Jesus Christ at His birth. It was a monumental event that caused seismic shifts throughout the world. We have stated that He was, and is, the only conceivable individual to fulfill every aspect of what was required to be Messiah. It was necessary that His birth be completed in every detail, as each prophecy was specific. A precise prophecy eliminated any attempt at false claims. Micah 5:2 prophesied the coming of Jesus Christ as Messiah by naming His birthplace: "But thou, Bethlehem Ephratah, though thou be little among the thousands of Judah, yet out of thee shall He come forth unto Me that is to be ruler in Israel."

This particular prophecy was accomplished by the events of Jesus' birth as seen in Luke 2:4-5 (KJV): "And Joseph also went up from Galilee, out of the city of Nazareth, into Judea, unto the city of David, which is called Bethlehem; (because he was of the house and lineage of David) to be taxed with Mary his espoused wife, being great with child." It is interesting to note that the decree of Caesar Augustus to tax the world launched the chain of events that fulfilled this one prophecy. As we have already reviewed Caesar's legacy, we must interject that God used Caesar without his knowing it.

Prophecies fulfilled by Christ established His existence and His claim as the Messiah. Several prophecies made a direct connection. The prophet Zechariah was instrumental in providing signs for recognizing the soon-coming Messiah. In Zechariah 9:9 (KJV), it is written, "Rejoice greatly, O daughter of Zion; shout, O daughter of Jerusalem: behold thy King cometh unto thee: He is just, and having salvation; lowly, and riding upon an ass, and upon a colt foal of an ass." Zechariah made it clear that the arrival and introduction of the Messiah would depict humility. Jesus fulfilled this prophecy, which identified Him as the Messiah, in Luke 19:35: "And they brought him to Jesus: and they cast their garments upon the colt, and they set Jesus thereon." Contemporary false messiahs, such as the Reverend Sun Myung Moon, cannot lay claim to having fulfilled this passage of Scripture. Their claims become even more impossible and improbable when we consider the description of the Messiah's death.

When we think of the Psalms, we are usually focused on King David. David recorded a lucid depiction of the death of the Messiah in Psalm 22:16 (KJV): "For dogs have compassed me: the assemblies of the wicked have enclosed me: they pierced my hands and feet." The aftermath of the Messiah's death is seen in Psalm 22:18 (KJV): "They part my garments among them, and cast lots upon my vesture." Jesus Christ fulfilled Psalm 22:16, as seen in Luke 23:33: "And when they were come to the place, which is called Calvary, there they crucified Him, and the malefactors, one on the right hand, and the other on the left." The fulfillment of Psalm 22:18 was established by three witnesses—Matthew, Mark, and John—as seen in Matthew 27:35, Mark 15:24, and John 19:24. John 19:24 records the scenario this way: "They said therefore among themselves, Let us not rend it, but cast lots for it, whose it shall be: that the Scripture might be fulfilled, which saith, They parted my raiment among them, and for My vesture they did cast lots."

Isaiah 53:5 bears a stark testimony to Jesus as Messiah: "But He was wounded for our transgressions, He was bruised for our iniquities: the chastisement of our peace was upon Him; and with His stripes we are healed." Additionally, Isaiah 53:7 (KJV) bears witness: "He was oppressed, and He was afflicted, yet He opened not His mouth: He is brought as a lamb to the slaughter, and as a sheep before her shearers is dumb, so He openeth not His mouth." Matthew 27:26 reports the fulfillment of Isaiah's prophecy, as found in Isaiah 53:5, when Jesus was ordered to be scourged by Pontius Pilate.

Isaiah 53:7 can be seen as fulfilled by Jesus in Matthew 27:12 (KJV): "And when He was accused of the chief priests and elders, He answered nothing." Matthew 27:13–14 (KJV) says, "Then said Pilate unto Him, Hearing Thou not how many things they witness against thee? And He answered him to never a word; insomuch that the governor marveled greatly." In fulfilling each prophecy, Jesus caused humanity to face reality and truth. Those who do not believe in Jesus Christ do not have knowledge of what the Word of God says about Him. This should form the basis of our approach when confronting nonbelievers. Fulfilled prophecies alone should be compelling enough evidence.

McIntosh and Twyman's unabridged edition of *The Archko Volume*, assembles evidence from witnesses who testified that Jesus, as the Son of God, rose from the dead. Official documents were made in the courts of Rome, and records from the Senatorial Docket are located in the Vatican. Recorded in the days of Jesus, they bear the testimonies of His generation. The crucifixion of Christ, and His subsequent resurrection, was of such importance that even Pontius Pilate and Caiaphas, the high priest, were compelled to record their findings. Indeed, they were the two responsible for Jesus' death. Pilate himself was required to make a complete report to the Roman emperor Tiberius Caesar upon the crucifixion and death of Jesus Christ. Pilate's encounter with the Nazarene impacted him to such a degree that he made his convictions known to Tiberius without reservation.

In *The Archko Volume*, Pilate was confronted with the truth, as he wrote to Caesar, "I am almost ready to say, as did Manlius at the cross, truly this was the Son of God" (p. 147). Pilate was a Roman official and governor appointed to uphold the laws of the Roman Empire. His near declaration, albeit short of absolute, was tantamount to treason, as Caesar alone was considered divine. Nevertheless, it was an extraordinary statement made by Pilate that gave tacit recognition of Christ's divinity as the Son of God. His letter was written during the most electrifying time in history: the resurrection of Christ.

The high priest Caiaphas was also seen as the authority who crucified Jesus, sending Him to His death by way of Pontius Pilate. Caiaphas was consigned to history as the judge who had malevolence in his heart. We must, however, look at the evidence contained in *The Archko Volume* once again, as a vindication of Caiaphas further validates the resurrection of Jesus Christ.

Caiaphas was compelled to send his letter of resignation to the Sanhedrim, the higher authoritative body of the Jewish nation, upon his declaration that he had seen the resurrected Christ. This one event changed him so dramatically that Caiaphas was torn as to whether his letter should be declared as a resignation or a confession. In *The Archko Volume*, Caiaphas asserted, "While thus engaged, with no one in the room but my wife and Annas, her father, when I lifted my eyes, behold Jesus of Nazareth stood before me" (p. 126). Caiaphas was confronted with the truth. Caiaphas further testified that Jesus had spoken to him, saying, "I died that you and all mankind might be saved" (p. 126).

Jesus was declared as "the Lamb slain from the foundation of the world." His purpose was to become the ultimate sacrifice for sin. Confronted by the resurrected Christ, Caiaphas knew that, as high priest, he could no longer make offerings or sacrifices for sin. Caiaphas acknowledged that if Jesus was the Messiah, the ruler they had been seeking, His influence would spread ever wider until the whole world acknowledged Him as Lord.

We have established the validity of Christ's claims through eyewitness accounts. As we have mentioned, He has left us a legacy of healing and counseling through His Holy Spirit, which continues today. We have also shown His fulfillment of prophecies recorded long before His arrival on earth. It is important to visit the impact that His legacy has left upon humanity and our modern civilization. We have already seen His powerful direction in the lives of great men and women of the past: George Washington, Dr. Martin Luther King Jr., the disciple Thomas, King David, and Esther. Additionally, there have been men and women of prominence whom we have not mentioned but whose lives have been impacted just as much: Abraham Lincoln, Joan of Arc, Aimee Semple McPherson, Smith Wigglesworth, Charles Finney, John and Charles Wesley, Billy Graham, and Watchman Nee, to name a few.

England was changed in the eighteenth century when John and Charles Wesley brought revival. They taught the simple gospel message of Jesus Christ, preaching that Jesus transformed lives. As England had drifted precipitously into a moral decay, the legacy of Christ—the salvation of humanity—transformed the core of England.

As the hearts of England's citizens changed, the nation itself reformed its laws, its schools, and its way of governing. Prisons that had been established for those deeply in debt were made illegal. Schools, universities, and hospitals became more readily accessible. Charities and religious orders were created to benefit society as a whole.

Hundreds of years ago, Africa was steeped in witchcraft, paganism, and cannibalism. As a result of missionaries having proclaimed the gospel message of Jesus Christ, Africa now boasts one of the fastest growing regions of new converts to Christianity in the world.

India was rife with Hinduism and pagan rituals when the disciple Thomas visited its shores. As a direct result of his efforts—and thousands of like-minded evangelists—India has expanded its Christian base by over a hundredfold. Today, Indian missionaries go around the world, proclaiming the good news that Jesus came to save humanity from their sins.

For thousands of years, China was ruled by feudalistic emperors. They were bent on enforcing ancestral worship and the teachings of Confucius and Buddha. When Mao Tse-tung captured power in 1948, his Communist government erased all forms of worship, creating a vacuum in search of divine assistance. Combined with the relentless efforts of thousands of missionaries over the years, that vacuum has produced the fastest growing Christian population on earth. Millions of underground believers have risked their lives to learn of the life of Jesus Christ and His teachings. Millions more have been transformed by His message.

Mao's godless communistic system produced famines across China. More than just spiritual famine, millions starved to death when his Red Army enforced purges across China through the Cultural Revolution. From 1966 until 1973, the Cultural Revolution eliminated Chinese suspected of having any Western influence. Underground Chinese Christians of Hunan Province faced the same purges and famine. They applied the principles of the Word of God and the teachings of Christ that they'd learned from foreign missionaries and smuggled copies of the Bible. Through active prayer, they were able to decrease the purges in their province that took place across the country. Additionally, they gave away a tenth of all the rice they grew, blunting the famine by feeding themselves and several surrounding Chinese provinces.

Nations, kings, and kingdoms have battled for the cause of Christ. The Crusades of the twelfth century created the legends of Saladin and King Richard the Lionhearted. Their war was fought in the name of two different gods. We remember a red cross on a field of white as the symbol that was flown on behalf of Jesus Christ during those turbulent times. That same emblem is used today by the charity that bears its name: the Red Cross.

The legacy of Christ is also found in the transformation of human hearts. Mary Magdalene washed the feet of Jesus, having an open heart transformed by His love. It was a demonstration that we can come to Christ just as we are. It also depicted Christ's love for us, showing that He will not turn us away under any circumstance, as long as we desire to come to Him of our own free will.

We are also reminded of one of the two thieves who hung on either side of Jesus as He was dying on the cross. One of the thieves must have recognized that Jesus represented life beyond the grave. Most assuredly, he knew that his own life that would soon end. His heart was transformed as he asked Jesus to remember him when He came into His kingdom. Jesus' response was to reassure him that he would be with Him in paradise on that very day. First, we recognize our new condition when our heart is changed. Later, we realize that Jesus is the only one able to complete that process.

Millions of people in every nation and culture have testified to the transforming power of Jesus Christ. Missionaries have experienced people of all races and nationalities coming to believe the salvation message of Christ. Healings, deliverances, and changing hearts have transcended boundaries and language barriers. The legacy of Christ has removed such hurdles and influenced the hearts of men to reach the lost.

The legacy of Christ is unique in that it is the only one that can boast of a resurrection. Of all the legacies we have covered and the personalities we have discussed, none have claimed to have risen from the dead or to have promised life after death. When Lazarus died, Jesus was approached by his sister Martha concerning the resurrection. She sought reassurance. Jesus provided the answer she needed by proclaiming in John 11:25–26 (KJV), "I am the resurrection, and the life: he that believeth in Me, though he were dead, yet shall he live: And whosoever liveth and believeth in Me shall never die. Believest thou this?"

Dr. David L. Clifton

When Jesus rose from the dead, it was an event that shook the Roman Empire to its very foundations. Rumors abounded that Jesus' disciples had taken His body. Soldiers had been posted at the tomb for fear that such a disappearance would spark frenzy among His followers. In Matthew 27:65–66 (KJV), we find the elaborate precautions that were taken to protect the body of Jesus and to prevent it from being taken. It records the following: "Pilate said unto them, Ye have a watch: go your way make it as sure as you can. So they went, and made the sepulcher sure, sealing the stone, and setting a watch."

A marble slab discovered in 1878 was purportedly inscribed as a decree by the emperor Claudius. Known as the Nazareth Decree, it prohibited the desecration or unsettling of graves, and the prescribed penalty for doing so was a death sentence. It is plausible that Claudius was aware of the fact that Christians believed that Jesus would rise from the dead. As we have mentioned before, Pontius Pilate found it necessary to report these events to the emperor Tiberius. Such was the atmosphere of the day.

Matthew 28:2 (KJV) highlights the drama of Jesus' resurrection further: "And, behold, there was a great earthquake: for the angel of the Lord descended from heaven, and came and rolled back the stone from the door, and sat upon it." Matthew 28:3–4 provides the climax: "His countenance was like lightning, and his raiment white as snow: And for fear of him the keepers did shake, and became as dead men."

The four Synoptic Gospels present the account of Jesus' resurrection somewhat differently from one another.

146

However, each author shared his unique perspective of the events that unfolded. All agreed that Jesus had risen, and they provided unique details explaining this awe-inspiring event. All that was recorded documented the greatest event ever to take place in history.

It is noteworthy that Jesus appeared to over five hundred witnesses after His resurrection from the dead. This group of witnesses provided for the proliferation of the gospel, and many eyewitness accounts proved that Jesus was alive. Furthermore, Jesus' resurrection electrified His followers into proclaiming that He was the Messiah, the Son of the living God. His legacy is summed up in His resurrection, for all that He did and all that He accomplished would have been in vain had He not risen.

So much more must be mentioned regarding the legacy of Christ. Here we must note His many, many miracles that caused so many to believe in Him. The miracle at Cana of Galilee, where Jesus turned the water into wine, was His first miracle. There was also the feeding of the five thousand, where the miracle of the fishes and loaves became widely known throughout the world. The healing of blind Bartimaeus was undoubtedly an event that must have stirred the imaginations of the masses far and wide. And we cannot forget the woman with the issue of blood; she was healed after having had an infirmity for eighteen years. The demon-possessed man who was set free by Jesus among the tombstones was another miracle.

And what are we to say of Lazarus, who was raised from the dead by the command spoken from Jesus? His testimony bore more weight than any other as to who Jesus was and why

He came. It was perhaps the greatest miracle among many that testified to Jesus being the Son of God and the Messiah spoken of in prophecy. It certainly affirmed His right to say, "I am the resurrection and the life."

The Beatitudes and the Lord's Prayer, given to us as an example of how we are to pray, are additional elements of the legacy of Jesus. How many churches, movies, meetings, and events have recited His words? We are reminded that Jesus said in Luke 21:33 (KJV), "Heaven and earth shall pass away: but My words shall not pass away." Jesus is probably quoted more often than any human that has lived on earth.

The facts we have ascertained prove that Jesus existed. His existence, in turn, and the prophetic events fulfilled by Him prove that He is the Messiah and the Son of God. We can now see that He has also given us healing, salvation, and eternal life. These were provided for us when He rose from the dead.

Jesus exemplified all that was perfect. He bore our sins and became a sacrifice for our sins, even though He was without sin. He taught us to love our neighbor as we love ourselves. And He showed us that the greatest commandment is to love the Lord God with all of our mind, soul, and heart.

11

Conclusion

We are compelled to conclude with an undeniable statement: that Jesus Christ left the greatest legacy of all. When comparing the legacy of God to the legacy of human beings, there is no contest. However, we have pointed out the characteristics of each person we have discussed, inevitably comparing them to those of Christ.

We have seen the legacy of kings, both good and bad. Notably, one ruler was a woman: Queen Esther. She proved to be exemplary in all that she accomplished. We have also seen monarchs of a dying era, clinging to traditional liturgical surroundings to preserve what remained of their empire. Additionally, we have traveled through history to see the rise of emperor worship during the Roman Empire. We have acknowledged man's attempt to replace his needs and wants with devices of his own creation.

We have seen what man can accomplish when he pursues his desires in accordance with God's will. We have seen followers of Christ who gave their very lives for His cause.

Passion and determination guided their every thought and action. We have also written of men of vision who pursued their dreams and goals to benefit humanity. Some became the defining image of their age through excellent leadership, ever acknowledging the source of their success as God Himself. We have also seen that even with all of their achievements, none of them could match the legacy of Jesus Christ.

We also wrote of men who failed to acknowledge God; theirs was a legacy created to self to promote their evil desires. As we have seen, Hitler and Nero left nothing but destruction and chaos along their paths. Elevation of their self-centered causes became their primary concern and overriding drive to dominate and subjugate the world. Their actions resulted in the termination of their desires, as well as their own lives.

We have seen the legacy of King David, founded upon the heart of a man after God's own heart. From his lineage came Jesus Christ. We have seen the legacy of Queen Esther, who was a type of Christ in her willingness to lay down her life for the lives of her people. The legacy of Constantine broadened Christianity.

Man's attempt to leave a lasting legacy is exemplified by Louis XIV and the caesars of the Roman Empire. We have seen that their legacies, as grand as they were, were of no eternal value. The Roman Empire itself lies in ruins. Likewise, we have seen the lives of Nicholas II and his wife Alexandra, who attempted to please God in every way in order to preserve what remained of their realm. What they needed most was the legacy of Christ and His offer of healing, counsel, and salvation.

Finally, we have seen the legacies of Dr. Martin Luther King Jr., George Washington, and the disciple Thomas, all followers of Christ who benefited humanity in some way.

But it was, and is, the legacy of Jesus Christ that provided eternal benefit for all people. His gift of salvation for eternal life, His healing for humanity, and His offer of counsel have left us a living legacy.

Bibliography

Bernier, Olivier. *Louis XIV, A Royal Life*. New York: Doubleday, 1987.

Levi, Anthony. *Louis XIV*. New York: Carroll and Graf Publishers, 2004.

The Bible, King James Version. Goodyear, Ariz.: GEM Publishing, 2001.

Hagin, Kenneth E. *Understanding the Anointing*. Tulsa, Okla.: Kenneth Hagin Ministries, Inc., 1983.

Webster's Seventh New Collegiate Dictionary. Springfield, Mass.: G. and C. Merriam Company, 1971.

Nelson's Illustrated Bible Dictionary. Nashville: Thomas Nelson, Inc., 1986.

The Ryrie Study Bible, New International Version. Chicago: Zondervan Bible Publishers, 1986.

Cottle, Ronald E. *Anointed to Reign*. Shippensburg, Pa.: Destiny Image Publishers, Inc., 1996.

Swindoll, Charles R. *David, a Man of Passion and Destiny*. Nashville: Word Publishing, 2000.

Meyer, F. B. *The Life of David*. Lynnwood, Washington: Emerald Books Publishing, 1995.

Getz, Gene A. David. *Seeking God Faithfully*. Nashville: Broadman and Holman Publishers, 1995.

Lockyer, Herbert. *All the Kings and Queens of the Bible*. Grand Rapids, Mich.: Zondervan Publishing House, 1961.

Hagin, Kenneth E. *A Fresh Anointing*. Tulsa, Okla.: Kenneth Hagin Ministries, Inc., 1997.

Richards, Larry O. *Every Man in the Bible*. Nashville: Thomas Nelson, Inc., 1999.

Davis, Dale Ralph. *Focus on the Bible, II Samuel: Out of Every Adversity*. Ross-shire, Great Britain: Christian Focus Publications, 1999.

Finnegan, Edward G. *New Webster's Thesaurus*. Washington, DC: DPC Publishing, 1987.

Nelson, Thomas. *The Holy Bible, New King James Version*. Nashville: Broadman & Holman Publishers, 1996.

Webster's New Collegiate Dictionary. Cambridge, Mass.: G & C Merriam Company, 1959.

Geisler, Norman L. *A Popular Survey of the Old Testament*. Grant Rapids, Mich.: Baker Books, 1977.

The Illustrated Bible Dictionary, Volume I. Sydney, Australia: Tyndale House Publishers, 1980.

Swindoll, Charles R. *Esther: A Woman of Strength and Dignity*. Nashville: Word Publishing, Inc., 1997.

Kurth, Peter. *The Lost World of Nicholas and Alexandra, Tsar*. Toronto, Ontario: Madison Press Books, 1995.

Massie, Robert K. *Nicholas and Alexandra*. Atheneum, New York: McClelland and Stewart Ltd., 1967.

Iroshnikov, Mikhail, Liudmila Protsai, and Yuri Shelayev. *The Sunset of the Romanov Dynasty*. Moscow, Russia: Pervaya Obraztsovaya Printing House, 1992.

Schuman, Michael A. *Martin Luther King Jr., Leader for Civil Rights*. Springfield, N.J.: Enslow Publishers, Inc., 1996.

Frady, Marshall. *Martin Luther King Jr.* New York: Penguin Group Publishing, 2002.

Franklin, Victor P. *Martin Luther Jr. Biography*. New York: Park Lane Press, 1998.

Damazio, Frank. *The Making of a Leader*. Portland, Ore.: City Bible Publishing, 1988.

King, Martin L. *Strength to Love*. Asheville, N.C.: Augsberg Fortress Publishers, 1989.

Grant, Michael. *The Roman Emperors*. New York: Charles Scribner's Sons, 1985.

Massie, Allan. *The Caesars*. New York: Martin Secker and Warburg Limited, 1983.

Barker, Kenneth, ed. *New International Version Study Bible*. Grand Rapids, Mich.: Zondervan Publishing House, 1995.

Lockyer, Herbert. *All the Apostles of the Bible*. Grand Rapids, Mich.: Zondervan Publishing House, 1972.

Peterson, Eugene H. *The Message*. Colorado Springs, Colo.: NavPress Publishing Group, 1995.

Scoffield, C. I., ed. *King James Scoffield Study Bible*. New York: Oxford University Press, 1945.

Henrichson, Walter A. *Disciples Are Made Not Born*. Colorado Springs, Colo.: SP Publications, Inc., 1988.

Getz, Gene A. *The Apostles Becoming Unified through Diversity*. Nashville: Broadman and Holman Publishers, 1998.

Barclay, William. *Jesus as They Saw Him*. Grand Rapids, Mich.: William B. Eerdmans Publishing Company, 1995.

Jeffrey, Grant R. *Jesus The Great Debate*. Toronto, Ontario: Frontier Research Publications, Inc., 1999.

Nystrom, Carolyn. *New Testament Characters*. Downers Grove, Ill.: Intervarsity Press, 1993.

Laird, Charlton. *Webster's New World Thesaurus*. Simon and Shuster, Inc., 1974.

Land, Richard. *For Faith and Family*. BeliefNet.com., 2003.

Rosenbaum, Ron. *Explaining Hitler*. New York: Random House, Inc., 1998.

Webster's New World Dictionary. New York and Cleveland, Ohio: The World Publishing Company, 1972.

Payne, Robert. *The Life and Death of Adolf Hitler*. New York: Praeger Publishers, 1973.

Whitney, David C. *The American Presidents*. Pleasantville, N.Y.: The Readers Digest Association, Inc., 1996.

Arkin, Marc. "The Federalist Brief." Posted 2004. *www.earstohear.net*.

Gibson, Mel. *The Passion*. Wheaton, Ill.: Icon Distribution, Inc., 2004.

The Bible, God's Holy Word, New International Version. Colorado Springs, Colo.: International Bible Society, 1984.

Pentecost, J. Dwight. *The Word and Works of Jesus Christ: A Study of the Life of Christ*. Grand Rapids, Mich.: Zondervan Publishing House, 1981.

Webster's New World Dictionary of the American Language. New York: World Publishing Company, 1972.

Haggard, Ted. *Primary Purpose*. Lake Mary, Fla.: Creation House, 1995.

King James Version of the Holy Bible. New York: Collins World Publishing, 1978.

Strong, James. *Strong's Exhaustive Concordance of the Bible*. Peabody, Mass.: Hendrickson Publishers, 1999.

Horton, T. C. *The Names of Christ*. Chicago: Moody Press, 1994.

The Holy Bible, Revised Version of 1881. Philadelphia: A. J. Holman and Company, 1881.

Rodale, Jerome Irving. *The Synonym Finder*. Emmaus, Pa., 1978.

The Holy Bible, New King James Version. Grand Rapids, Mich.: National Publishing Company, 1982.

Lindsay, Gordon. *The Life and Teachings of Christ*. Dallas, Tex.: Christ for the Nations, Inc., 1999.

Hill, Craig. *The Ancient Paths*. Littleton, Colo.: Family Foundation Publishing, 1992.

The New Merriam-Webster Dictionary. Springfield, Mass.: Merriam-Webster Publishing, Inc., 1989.

The Bible, Revised Standard Version. New York: American Bible Society, 1980.

Bosworth, Fred Francis. *Christ the Healer*. Grand Rapids, Mich.: Fleming H. Revell Publishing, Inc., 1973.

Gehlhar, Philip. *Healing from Cancer and All Other Diseases*. Anaheim, Calif.: Pace Publication Arts, 1997.

Hickey, Marilyn. *Be Healed*. Denver: Marilyn Hickey Ministries, Inc., 1992.

Price, Frederick K. *Is Healing For All?* Tulsa, Okla.: Harrison House Publishing, Inc., 1976.

Promises from God's Word. Grand Rapids, Mich.: Word Publishing, Inc., 1996.

Kenyon, E. W. *The Blood Covenant*. Lynnwood, Wash.: Kenyon's Gospel Publishing Society, 1997.

Hagin, Kenneth E. *Seven Things You Should Know about Divine Healing*. Tulsa, Okla.: Faith Library Publications, 1979.

Allen, James. *As a Man Thinketh*. New York: Grosset and Dunlap Publishing, Inc., 1930.

Feltman, John. *Healing Remedies and Techniques*. New York: The Berkeley Publishing Group, 1996.

McIntosh and Twyman, trans. *The Archko Volume*. New Canaan, Conn.: Keats Publishing, Inc., 1975.